GOD ONLINE

A Mystic's Guide to the Internet

BRUCE G. EPPERLY

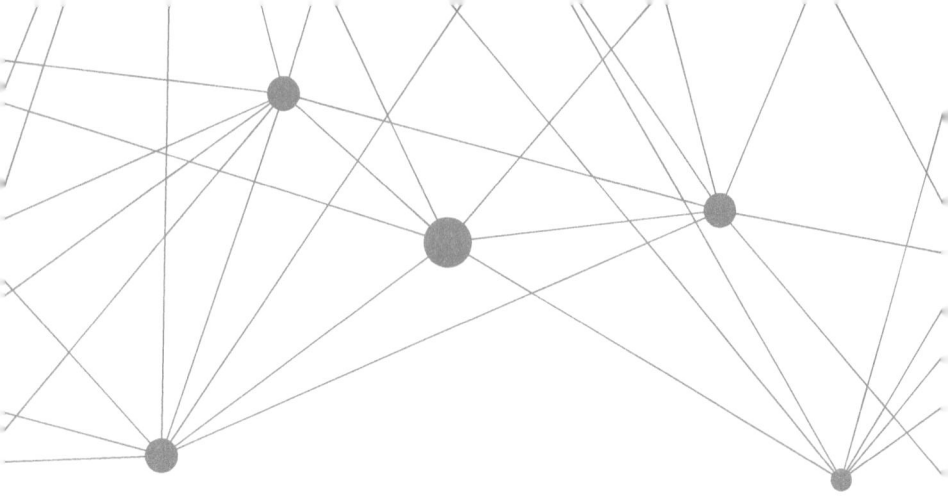

GOD ONLINE

A Mystic's Guide to the Internet

BRUCE G. EPPERLY

ANAMCHARA
BOOKS

Copyright © Bruce G. Epperly, 2020.

ANAMCHARA BOOKS
Vestal, New York 13850
www.AnamcharaBooks.com

All Scripture quotations, unless otherwise indicated, are from the New Revised Standard Version Bible, copyright © 1989 the Division of Christian Education of the National Council of the Churches of Christ in the United States of America. Used by permission. All rights reserved. Scripture quotation marked HCSB is from the Holman Christian Standard Bible,® copyright © 1999, 2000, 2002, 2003, 2009 by Holman Bible Publishers. Used by permission. Scripture quotations marked NASB are from the New American Standard Bible,® copyright © 1960, 1962, 1963, 1968, 1971, 1972, 1973, 1975, 1977, 1995 by The Lockman Foundation. Used by permission. www.Lockman.org. Scripture quotations marked NIV are from the Holy Bible, New International Version®, NIV,® copyright © 1973, 1978, 1984, 2011 by Biblica, Inc.® Used by permission. All rights reserved worldwide. Scripture quotations marked NLT are from the Holy Bible, New Living Translation, copyright © 1996, 2004, 2015 by Tyndale House Foundation. Used by permission of Tyndale House Publishers, Inc., Carol Stream, Illinois 60188. All rights reserved.

IngramSpark Paperback ISBN: 978-1-62524-786-5

Cover design by Micaela Grace.
Interior design by Micaela Grace.
Geometric line illustration by Berya113 (Dreamstime.com).

CONTENTS

Logging On: A Synchronous Invitation   9

1. The Sacrament of the Present Moment:
   Jean-Pierre de Caussade   19

2. Practicing the Presence of God on the Internet:
   Brother Lawrence   29

3. Listening to Your Life: *Frederick Buechner*   43

4. Daily Attentiveness: *Ignatius of Loyola*   55

5. Peace Is Every Post: *Thich Nhat Hanh*   67

6. Doing Ordinary Things with Love:
   Therese of Lisieux   79

7. Something Beautiful for God:
   Saint Teresa of Calcutta   91

8. Pause, Notice, and Respond: *Gerald May*   103

9. Prophetic Posting: *Howard Thurman*   113

10. What Is Your Vision for Your Unique and
    Unrepeatable Life?: *Mary Oliver*   189

LOGGING ON
A Synchronous Invitation

May the words of my mouth
and the meditation of my heart
be pleasing to you,
O Lord, my rock and my redeemer.
(Psalm 19:14 NLT)

Every book has a story, and my reflections on the spirituality of the Internet have a story, too. On July 3, 2019, Ellyn Sanna, publisher of Anamchara Books, asked me if I would consider writing a book on spiritual practices related to the Internet and social media. Being introverted and reflective by disposition, my initial response was, "Let me think about it." I had enough on my plate as a Cape Cod pastor, seminary professor, husband, and grandparent, and I was in the middle of another writing project. Still, I responded as I always do when some new and unexpected possibility comes into my life: I prayed about it, let my mind wander, and visualized how this project might nurture my own spirituality and the spiritual lives of those who might encounter the text. The Internet is at the heart of most our lives and has shaped my own scholarship, ministry, and friendships and the thought of being more intentional about my Internet practices was intriguing.

I went to bed that night as I always do, asking for guidance for the morning's writing and ministerial encounters. The next morning my prayers were answered. As I took my sunrise walk on Craigville Beach on Cape Cod, a flood of ideas began to cascade and constellate, giving me the green light to say "yes" to the project. In the spirit of Frederick Buechner's understanding of vocation, I felt an intersection between my deep gladness and intellectual passion and the spiritual needs of my companions on social media. I also felt that I needed to deepen my own spiritual connection with social media. I need to heal my approach to Internet and social media communications.

I placed one condition on myself: this book would have to be a laboratory for my own spiritual practices and mindful use of social media. My writing would have to connect with my own spiritual challenges with social media, and my quest to make it a sacrament of wisdom and community rather than a maelstrom of division and incivility. I made a personal vow that my conversations on Facebook and other social media platforms would become part of my daily practice of Examen, a mindful reflection on how my participation in these media would bring me closer to or further from God's vision for my life. I wanted to let go of my own attachments and my own need to be right, so that I might make my use of the Internet sacramental, a way of growing spiritually rather than succumbing to my worst emotions. My goal was to embody the graceful interdependence of life in my Internet communications.

Writing a text on the spirituality of the Internet and social media would be personal and concrete, rather than abstract and academic. I would vow to become more prayerful, intentional, and self-aware in my social-media practices. My use of various forms of online media would become a prayer form, authentic to my values and experience. Although I would at times be prophetic and challenging in my posts and communications, my quest was to be congruent with God's moment-to-moment vision for my life. I would emphasize the sanctuary of private contemplation as the ground of public communication. I wanted the Internet to be a gateway to God, a thin place, as the Celts assert, where heaven and earth meet, and the world is transformed. I sought spiritual integrity, so that words and meditations in daily life and on the Internet would be in sync, both reflecting my desire to be faithful to God's vision in every encounter.

My need for mindfulness became obvious the morning I chose to begin this spiritual adventure. The Fourth of July 2019 was a particularly contentious day on social media, with Facebook friends arguing with one another and name-calling about the Trump administration's treatment of undocumented immigrants, most especially the separation of young children from their parents on our borderlands, and the audacity of Donald Trump's coopting Fourth of July festivities on the Washington DC Mall with a program of his own, complete with tanks and a military flyover. Invectives and derisive comments were the order of the day both from the right and left sides of the political spectrum. It was all I could do not to get caught up in the chaos of incivility. But I paused, recognizing that my goal was to be a voice of healing, grounded in fact and civil discourse, and not an agent of division and denunciation.

On that July 4, 2019, I decided to make a commitment to join prayer and contemplation with my involvement in social media so that, as the psalmist might have said were he (or she) alive today, "the words of my posts and meditation of my heart would be acceptable to God" and in alignment with God's millisecond-by-millisecond inspirational movements in my life. This book is the fruit of my spiritual adventures with social media in the months that followed.

As I pondered the wisdom of Psalm 19, I discovered that my words and meditations were part of a larger spiritual tapestry touching every aspect of my life and my relationship with all creation. For our Hebraic forerunners, like the sages of the Hindu holy book the Vedas, words were creative and world shaping. The psalmist began the hymn from Psalm 19 with words proclaiming a universe of praise, embracing the non-human and human worlds. The psalmist's chant joins the music of the spheres in proclaiming God's artistry and wisdom flowing through all things:

> The heavens declare the glory of God;
> the skies proclaim the work of his hands.
> Day after day they pour forth speech;
> night after night they reveal knowledge.
> They have no speech, they use no words;
> no sound is heard from them.

> Yet their voice goes out into all the earth,
> their words to the ends of the world.
> (Psalm 19:1–4 NIV)

The psalmist recognizes that our words and deeds emerge from a cosmic context as well as our individual reflections. Our personal creativity reflects the movements of the evolving universe, aiming, as the philosopher Alfred North Whitehead asserts, at the production of beauty. What we do as artists, writers, speakers, parents, friends, and grandparents arises from and contributes to the world around us. Not bound to the past, God nurtures novelty and adventure in the present moment and emerging future. Still, our adventures come to fruition in an orderly and evolving universe, embodying in greater or lesser degrees "the moral arc" aiming at Shalom—a world of wholeness, healing, and peace.

> The instructions of the Lord are perfect,
> reviving the soul.
> The decrees of the Lord are trustworthy,
> making wise the simple.
> The commandments of the Lord are right,
> bringing joy to the heart.
> The commands of the Lord are clear,
> giving insight for living.
> Reverence for the Lord is pure,
> lasting forever.
> The laws of the Lord are true;
> each one is fair.
> (Psalm 19:7–9 NLT)

God's law is relational and not legalistic, intending to promote wisdom, reconciliation, and community. The "fear of the Lord"—what Rabbi Abraham Joshua Heschel calls radical amazement—reminds us that God is God and we aren't. Our deepest beliefs and practices, whether religious or political, are finite, imperfect, and subject to constant creative transformation.

Though written twenty-five hundred years before the emergence of the Worldwide Web, the words of Psalm 19 have become an anchor for my social media practices. The psalmist's affirmations raised questions for my own spiritual examinations: Is God moving through my social media platforms and posts? Can I discern God's presence in posts that edify and disturb me? Do my words and meditations reflect Divine wisdom? Do they enlighten and encourage? Do they bring joy as well as challenge to those with whom I interact? Do they manifest and promote the glory of God? Can I experience the quest for God in my posts and in the often-unsettling posts of companions on social media?

Today, we find ourselves living in what Jesuit spiritual teacher-paleontologist Teilhard de Chardin described as the "noosphere," the dynamic sphere of thought encircling and connecting the Earth. We are all joined in this intricate web of relatedness, both metaphysically and technologically. The interdependence of life, manifest in today's communications media, is ambiguous in nature, as Teilhard recognizes. What joins us in the "mind of Christ," uniting humankind in common cause as God's companions in evolution, can also divide us, diabolically separating us into siloes of contention and incivility. Yet, beneath the many contrasting, and often conflicting, voices of social media, the psalmist's words ring true. There is a deeper interdependence that gracefully orients us toward a dynamic balance of community and individuality, unity and diversity. In the spirit of the butterfly effect, our words radiate across the universe, bringing harmony and healing—or contributing to chaos and disorder.

The ubiquity of social media reflects Teilhard's vision of the noospheric impact of technology. We have become cells in a planetary mind, joined by communications technology as well as Divine creativity. Non-local causation manifests itself when we sign into Facebook, Twitter, Instagram, Pinterest, and any other social media platform. The impact of our participation in the noosphere, the synergetic planetary mind, can nurture or detract from the well-being of ourselves and persons across the globe.

As we use these social media platforms, we need to remember another kind of non-locality, the intricate connectedness of our prayerful spiritual practices. Prayer connects us immediately, positively, and non-locally across the planet and the universe, creating life-enhancing fields of force around those for whom we pray. Prayer awakens the energies of love that can transform cells as well as souls. The obvious implication in terms of noospheric technology is that joining prayer and social media reflects God's providence in an age of immediate technological communication. In the course of reflecting on the spirituality of the Internet, I have come to realize that my goal is to experience God online, and to log into God as I log onto the Internet.

Jewish mysticism notes that the world is saved one soul at a time. Each soul's healing contributes to the healing of the universe and our ultimate reconnection with the primal unity of creation. Perhaps the world is saved one act, one click, or one post at a time. When we do ordinary things with great love, as Therese of Lisieux counsels, we bring beauty and healing to our companions on the Internet and to the planetary mind. The omnipresent God is as near as the next key stroke, the next post or response to another's online comment.

We need a whole-person spirituality grounded in a sense of the holiness of all creation and reverence for life despite the conflicts that characterize our world. A spirit at peace reveals itself in compassionate communications, strong and direct at times but always aimed at healing and wholeness and reconciliation, despite differences of perspective. We can advocate vigorously for our position and challenge others' viewpoints without dehumanizing and denigrating them.

In the course of our Internet reflections, our noospheric adventure will be inspired by the wisdom of the Christian mystical tradition. The mystics we will encounter will guide our daily lives as well as our Internet interactions. Civility on social media relates to the totality of our lives, not just our social media interactions. Our Internet daily commitments reflect our willingness to go beyond self-interest and ego gratification to world loyalty and generosity, and to claim our vocation as God's companions in healing the world. In reflecting on the mystics described in this text, we will discover that we too are mystics who can encounter God on the Internet.

Each chapter's dialogue with a mystic will conclude with a spiritual practice that will enable us to discover, in the spirit of the patriarch Jacob's exclamation, that "God is online, and we did not know it." Hopefully you will recognize the importance of stillness and self-awareness as the inspiration to communication and honor the womb of creative wisdom in your own life.

I am grateful to Ellyn Sanna, the creative and inspirational publisher of Anamchara Books, who invited me to write this book, and to my Internet and social media colleagues who shared their experiences of finding God online. I am grateful even to those social media companions whose opinions push all my buttons. They, too, have been my teachers, enabling me to choose the pathways of prophetic healing and peaceful challenge. I invite you to join me in a holy adventure that will bring light and love to your postings and reading—and awaken the spirit of unity with all creation one post at a time.

FINDING GOD ON THE INTERNET
How to Practice an Internet Examen

The "Examen" or "examination of conscience," popularized by Ignatius of Loyola, the parent of the Jesuits, is a simple but profound process that asks that we listen to our spiritual lives, noting the quality of our experience and response to God's presence in our lives.

The point of the Examen is self-awareness and personal transformation. We give thanks for moments of grace and vow to amend behaviors that distance us from God and our neighbor. In an updated form of the Examen, appropriate to twenty-first-century persons, we begin with a time of contemplative stillness. After a time of silent opening to Divine wisdom, we then focus on the following:

- Gratitude for God's presence in our life and throughout the day.
- Gratitude for the gifts of the Internet and social media.
- Areas in which we have experienced God's intimacy throughout the day.
- Areas in which we have experienced God's nearness on the Internet and social media.
- Areas in which we have strayed from God's vision throughout the day and in our use of the Internet and social media.
- Commitment to following God's vision for our life, especially our use of the Internet and social media.
- Prayerful placement of our future in God's care, asking for Divine guidance in the day ahead.
- Prayer for ways to use the Internet for the glory of God and the well-being of our neighbor.
- Discernment of a concrete and active step we can make to be more faithful to God's vision for our involvement in the Internet and social media.

We conclude with a few minutes of silence and a prayer such as:

God of technological creativity, whose wisdom and imagination embodied in human creativity gave birth to social media, awaken me to your vision of Shalom. Let your planetary vision guide my interactions on the Internet and social media, so that every message glorifies you and brings truth and beauty to those with whom I communicate. I give thanks for my social media friends and pray that they may experience your joy in their lives. Bless my fingers as I type. Trusting your Loving Wisdom to be much greater than my own, may the words of my mouth and meditations of my heart be acceptable in your sight, O God, my companion, guide, and inspiration. Amen.

One

THE SACRAMENT OF THE PRESENT MOMENT

Jean-Pierre de Caussade

The true light,
which enlightens everyone,
was coming into the world.

(John 1:9)

You are seeking God, dear sister,
and God is everywhere.
Everything proclaims God to you,
everything reveals God to you,
everything brings God to you.

**God is by your side,
over you and around and in you.**

**The books the Holy Spirit
is writing are living,
and every soul a volume
in which the divine author
makes a true revelation of his world,
explaining it to every heart,
unfolding it in every moment.**[1]

(Jean-Pierre de Caussade)

Ralph Waldo Emerson once told an audience of Harvard Divinity School graduates, "You are a bard of the Holy Ghost." Emerson's affirmation that all spiritual leaders could channel God's revelation for their place and time was controversial to those who saw humans as "sinners in the hands of an angry God" and who believed that God predestined some to salvation and others to damnation. For Emerson, however, God spoke through finite and imperfect humanity in its entirety, providing revelations appropriate to our time and place. The true light, as John's Gospel asserts, shines on everyone even when we turn our attention to darkness (John 1:9). Even in our darkness, we receive Divine light.

A hundred years before Emerson, Jesuit spiritual guide Jean-Pierre de Caussade (1675–1751) proclaimed a ubiquitous circle of revelation, telling his readers that the Holy Spirit was speaking within their lives, making each person either a hidden or revealed word of God. Can you imagine that—the Holy Spirit guiding you as you log on to your e-mail or sign on to Twitter or Facebook? Can you visualize your postings as being guided by the Holy Spirit? How would that shape the quality of your interactions on the Internet? What if you experienced every encounter, including those on the Internet, as windows into wonder, opportunities for what Abraham Joshua Heschel described as radical amazement?

Throughout my quest to live spiritually on the Internet, I have pondered the following questions: Does the Spirit speak on the Internet and through my personal Internet notifications? Can we encounter the Holy One on Facebook, Instagram, Twitter, and all the other social media apps? Within the storms of contention and incivility, can we discern the still, small voice of God? Do the voices of discord, even those who challenge or troll our posts, also reveal something of God for those who have eyes to see and ears to hear? In the spirit of the television series *God Friended Me*, can our online adventures enhance our friendship with God and one another and share in God's aim at healing the world? Does the Spirit speak through me, inviting my social media companions to claim their own

> **The present moment is always full of infinite treasure. It contains far more than you can possibly grasp.**
>
> *(Jean-Pierre de Caussade)*

unique gifts of the Spirit? Do even the most contentious persons reveal something of Divinity, disguised by their anxiety and antipathy?

In a God-filled universe, somehow the answer to each of my queries must be "yes." God enlightens, incognito, even those who seek darkness. The Holy One loves those who choose alienation rather than community. As part of God's enlightenment project, I need to devote my online postings to advancing God's healing vision.

I seek to live by the following affirmation: "Wherever I am, I reflect and channel God's blessings." Now that's a tall order and I often fail, succumbing to impatience and judgment of those I presume to be "lesser mortals," whether on social media, the highway, or in the White House. Still I seek, despite my failures, to bless individual encounters, community events, and political activi-ties. While I continue to post articles that provoke back-and-forth conversation among contrasting positions, my goal is to bless these media as well as promote civility and friendship across varied political and social perspectives.

And yet, can I bless and challenge at the same time? That is the question for many of us, isn't it?

Being a bard of the Holy Ghost on social media requires a good deal of mindfulness and self-control. Often, I need to resist correcting a false statement or engaging in a verbal joust with someone who is likely unpersuadable to my viewpoint. In any given morning, among my diverse community of Facebook friends, I observe as many as fifty false, misleading, or defamatory comments. Facts and the quest for truth is essential for spiritual integrity and I want always to speak the truth. Accordingly, I regularly check many of these comments on reputable online sources such as NPR, PBS, Snopes, and PolitiFact, and I never post a secondhand statement without verification from reliable sources. Sometimes I write a witty, erudite, and scathing response to a Facebook post—and then I take a breath and invoke one of my Internet mantras: "Don't press send." I get my vitriol or sense of superiority

> **Souls who can recognize God in the most trivial, the most grievous and the most mortifying things that happen to them in their lives, honor everything equally with delight and rejoicing, and welcome with open arms what others dread and avoid.**
>
> *(Jean-Pierre de Caussade)*

out of my system in the process of writing, and then I delete and let go, recognizing that fueling the fire of contention does no good to my spirit or to the well-being of those whom I seek to correct. Of course, I do challenge racist or other hate-fueled memes posted by my Christian siblings, asking questions such as, "Is this congruent with your faith? Do you think Jesus would describe another person this way? What would Jesus say in this situation? Would Jesus support this political policy?"

Social media provides many humorous and unexpected encounters. Recently, I found myself in conversation with what my Facebook colleagues later identified as a Russian troll, possibly a bored Russian programmer sitting in a Moscow warehouse. I assumed that the troll was an authentic social media companion, because, sadly, his behavior was not unusual for Internet conversations. Many people on social media quickly move from disagreement to denunciation and conversation to name-calling.

I "unfriended" the troll, although as I looked back at our thread of conversations, I was pleased that I maintained a civil and rational approach to our interactions.

Given how much time many of us spend on social media, the quality of our spiritual lives depends on bringing our highest selves to our Internet interactions. Jean-Pierre de Caussade's affirmation of the sacrament of the present moment inspires me to recognize that God is addressing us through every encounter. God's intimate presence in my life invites me to consider the sacramental nature of social media. As Abraham Lincoln noted, we need to bring the better angels of our nature to every encounter, whether in the marketplace or online. Is it possible for me to make the Internet a temple of the Holy Spirit, a sacrament of words and images?

> **What God arranges for us to experience at each moment is the best and holiest thing that could happen to us.**
>
> *(Jean-Pierre de Caussade)*

A creative interpretation of the Genesis myth of the fall of humankind, the story of Adam and Eve, illuminates the evolution of social media. When I first signed up with Facebook in 2009, I saw it as a platform for celebrating the joys of everyday life. I posted photos of my family, woodlands, and beaches, and invitations to lectures and concerts. I shared news of books, articles, and blogs. At the time, I saw social media as profoundly incarnational. In celebrating the ordinary yet amazing moments of life, everyday life became a shrine revealing the holiness of each moment. While there was a good deal of narcissistic posting, social media pointed to the incredible reality of being alive. It highlighted our gratitude for life's simple pleasures and the people whose love have shaped our lives. Social media gave us an opportunity to reconnect with old friends and support persons facing personal challenges. But, like the fall of humankind, soon we were forced from the age of innocence.

What was intended to connect became the source of division. Like the first couple described in the legends of Genesis, our misuse of social media has banished us from the garden of relational celebration. Celebrating the ordinary was replaced by scorched-earth communication, dishonesty, and denunciation. Facebook friends became enemies, unfriending one another as a result of political and cultural differences.

> **All that takes place within us, around us, or through us, contains and conceals divine action.**
>
> *(Jean-Pierre de Caussade)*

In the wake of controversies over social media incivility, the misuse of data, election meddling, and trolling from foreign agencies, Facebook has released several commercials reminding its users of the origins of social media. Images of friendship, marriage, joyful times, and civil conversations are highlighted as the vision of social interactions, inviting us to return to that time of innocence when a "friend" meant friendship.

Genesis reports that the primordial couple could never return to the garden of innocence. Nor can we! We can, however, follow the example of the legendary Adam and Eve and give birth to new possibilities of tending the garden of social media. We can reclaim social media for joyful affirmation and prophetic healing.

> **The duties of each moment are the shadows beneath which hides the divine operation.**
>
> (Jean-Pierre de Caussade)

Our fall from innocence can be a fall upward toward spiritual maturity as we discover creative ways to use the Internet to promote community, reconciliation, and healing.

What would it be like to approach our social media and Internet interactions in the spirit of Jean-Pierre de Caussade's counsel? What would it be like to see the Internet as a sacramental media, consecrated for service and healing?

> Everything proclaims God to you,
> everything reveals God to you,
> everything brings God to you.
> God is by your side, over you and around and in you.

Can you imagine someone whose political and social viewpoints differ from your perspective as a manifestation of the Spirit? Can you imagine Divine light, peeking out from persons who perpetuate fake news and incivility? Can you seek holiness disguised by offensive political affiliations?

FINDING GOD ON THE INTERNET
Praying with the Spirit

Jean-Pierre de Caussade asserted that the Holy Spirit is writing a book with your life. In that same spirit, Ralph Waldo

Emerson described spiritual seekers as "bards of the Holy Ghost," whose lives are artistic creations in partnership with God. As you consider these concepts, what spiritual messages or Divine poetry will you post on social media?

The Affirmative Option

Guided by the Spirit, we learn to say "yes" to life in all its wonder, complexity, and challenge. We make our lives affirmations of grace, recognizing evil and chaos in the context of a deeper movement of Providence, the moral arc moving us toward reconciliation.

Following the guidance of Emerson and de Caussade, I invite you to begin by living with the following spiritual affirmations, repeating them several times each day and invoking them as you log on to social media and post your viewpoint, memes, or links to articles:

God's Spirit is inspiring my creativity.

I am an artist of God's Spirit.

In the course of the day, breathe deeply, visualizing God's lively breath filling you with each breath you take. Then exhale beauty and love into the world. You might use an affirmation grounded in Congregationalist pastor and spiritual guide Allan Armstrong Hunter's counsel:

I breathe the Spirit deeply in
And blow it gratefully out again.

TENDING THE GARDEN

First-American sages affirmed that we walk in beauty. Following their footsteps, I invite you to tend the garden of social media by posting positive messages and photographs. Yes, there is good reason to challenge injustice and incivility, and we are mandated to do so. We are also mandated to share out of our gratitude for the beauty of the Earth and the amazing realities of life itself, embodied in our daily lives of parenting, grandparenting, sharing meals, reading books, and serving the community. Celebrate daily wonders in the course of your social media posting.

As part of your social media mindfulness, you might repeat the following prayer or let the Spirit inspire you to create one of your own.

Prayer of Awareness and Transformation

Spirit of the Living God, fill me with your love. Let every breath awaken my sense of gratitude and wonder, and join me with all creation. Enlighten my mind and open my heart. Let me experience and embrace the holiness of this present moment. Let my words and meditations, my posts and communications, bring insight, healing, and beauty to the world. Amen.

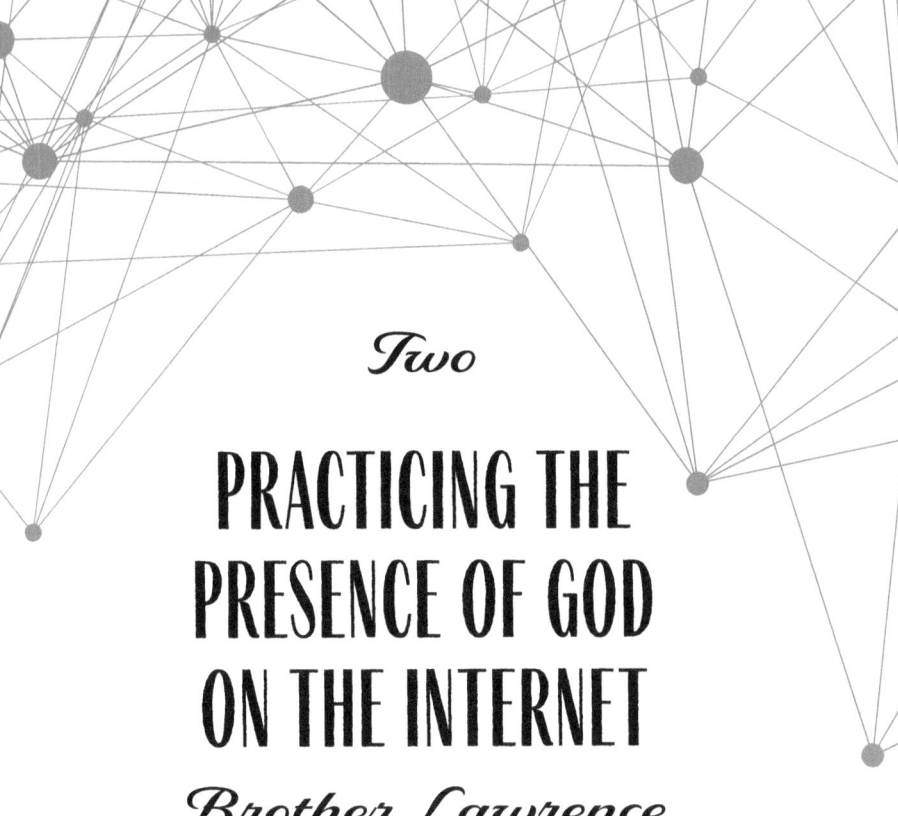

Two

PRACTICING THE PRESENCE OF GOD ON THE INTERNET

Brother Lawrence

Abram traveled through the land as far as the site of the great tree of Moreh at Shechem. At that time the Canaanites were in the land. The Lord appeared to Abram and said, "To your offspring I will give this land." So he built an altar there to the Lord, who had appeared to him. From there he went on toward the hills east of Bethel and pitched his tent, with Bethel on the west and Ai on the east. There he built an altar to the Lord and called on the name of the Lord.

(Genesis 12:6–8 NIV)

If I were a preacher,
I would preach nothing but practicing
the presence of God.[2]

All we have to do is to recognize God
as being intimately present within us.
Then we may speak
directly to God to ask for help,
to know the Divine will
in moments of uncertainty,
and to do whatever God wants
in a way that pleases God. . . .
This continuous conversation
should also include

> praising and loving God incessantly for the infinite goodness and perfection of the Divine.[3]
>
> *(Brother Lawrence)*

One of the most pervasive characteristics of contemporary North American life is the belief that we are self-determining individuals who can freely determine what is best and can go it alone without consulting God or our neighbors. We emphasize rights—how we can use our private property, resources, and firearms—without regard to our responsibilities to the common good and the well-being of neighbors and family. Personal freedom, whether in gun ownership, property rights, business practices, or the Internet, trumps the well-being of others.

This same disregard for the interdependence of life and our impact on others shapes our behavior on social media. We believe that we have the right to say whatever we want and to whomever we want on the Internet, especially to people we've never met whose opinions differ from our own. Others' feelings have little

> When we end our conversation with God by thinking of trivial nonsense and idle untruths, we cloud our hearts. Feed and nourish your soul with thoughts of God.[4]
>
> *(Brother Lawrence)*

importance compared to our right to share our own opinions or post on our Facebook page or Twitter stream.

We maintain the illusion of independence and choice, when in truth we are dependent on God, the environment, and the care of others for our survival and personal flourishing. There are no self-made persons in an interdependent universe. We shape each other and are shaped by every encounter and relationship. In the "body of Christ" (1 Corinthians 12), we all need one another's unique gifts and support to ensure the well-being of both the part and the whole. "If one member suffers, all the members suffer with it; if one member is honored, all the members rejoice with it." (1 Corinthians 12:26 NAS) What we say and do, and how we express our opinions, radiates across the noosphere, the intricately interdependent web of life that surrounds and permeates our planet. If a butterfly flapping its wings on Cape Cod can contribute to a thunderstorm in Pacific Grove, California, a toxic or uncivil tweet can depress the spiritual temperature of our nation.

Four hundred years ago, Brother Lawrence (1614–1691), born as George Herman, spoke of the heart of spirituality as the practice of the presence of God. This lay Carmelite monk discovered that he could serve God as fully in the kitchen as in the sanctuary and that he experienced God's presence as much while preparing meals for his fellow monks as he did in the monastery's worship services. Herman lived in a God-filled world in which every moment was an invitation to share in God's mission by serving his companions as well as unexpected strangers. According to a contemporary of Brother Lawrence:

Since loving God and loving one's neighbor are really the same thing, Brother Lawrence regarded those around him with the same affection he felt for the Lord. He believed that this was what Christ expressed in the Gospel: that anything he did for even the humblest of his brothers would be counted as being done for Jesus. He was particularly careful to serve his brothers, no matter what he was doing, and especially when he was working in the kitchen. There he treated them as if they were angels, a charity that he inspired in all those who succeeded him.[5]

For Brother Lawrence, every moment was an opportunity to praise God and receive Divine guidance. Recognizing our fallibility, we need God's wisdom for every task, not just to ensure our own spiritual well-being but to contribute to the spiritual well-being of others. I can imagine Brother Lawrence beginning his day, asking God to help him see Christ's presence in each person he met and to speak words of grace and healing, regardless of the tumult of the monastery's kitchen and refectory. I visualize Brother Lawrence singing God's praises throughout the day, humming a chant or singing a hymn as his moment-by-moment mantra, keeping his mind on Jesus regardless of the behavior of his

> **The practice of the Divine Presence is a natural and ongoing conversation with God, one that constantly occupies our minds with love and adoration for the infinite perfection of God.**
>
> *(Brother Lawrence)*

fellow monks. I contemplate him holding his tongue in response to a grumpy monk's comments, recognizing that his words could add to the angelic or demonic dimensions of life around him. Like Abraham and Sarah, he built altars of prayer wherever he found himself, recognizing that he was always on holy ground.

This morning, as I set out for my morning walk on Craigville and Covell's Beaches in my Cape Cod village, Brother Lawrence inspired me to words of praise. Despite my news feed's account of Amazon fires, tropical hurricanes, and another mass shooting in the United States, all the result in greater or lesser degree from human choices, the words of Baptist minister Robert Lowry's "How Can I Keep From Singing" filled my heart and leapt from my tongue as I took my solitary sunrise walk:

> My life flows on in endless song;
> Above earth's lamentation,
> I hear the sweet, though far-off hymn
> That hails a new creation;
> Through all the tumult and the strife
> I hear the music ringing;
> It finds an echo in my soul—
> How can I keep from singing?

In words apropos to the maelstrom of toxicity on the Internet and in the twitter storms of national leaders, Lowry continues his sung prayer:

> What though my joys and comforts die?
> The Lord my Saviour liveth;

> What though the darkness gather round?
> Songs in the night he giveth.
> No storm can shake my inmost calm
> While to that refuge clinging;
> Since Christ is Lord of heaven and earth,
> How can I keep from singing?

My hymn of praise was not an escapist plea to be rid of political concerns and care for the vulnerable, but a commitment to recognize that God's moral vision is at the work in the universe and that I have a part to play in healing the world. On that Sunday morning, I wondered as I began the day, *Do I hear God's music ringing and echoing in my soul? How can I, even in these tumultuous times, keep a song in my heart? How can I claim Lowry's call to keep singing God's song in this very strange and perilous time?*

> **Surrender yourself to God and you will find great joy. If you have truly surrendered yourself, you will be equally at peace in both suffering and pleasure.**
>
> *(Brother Lawrence)*

The words "no storm can shake my inmost calm" seemed appropriate this morning as I read the comments of a stranger in response to a Facebook post. Objecting to my post in support of humane treatment of children on the U.S. borderlands, he referred to me as "a libtard." As you might expect, I was tempted to defend my position in the strongest of terms, perhaps resorting to an expletive of my own. Instead, I took a breath, "blocked" him from further posts, and deleted his post.

Spiritual equanimity and civility are not invitations to abuse by others or the acceptance of inappropriate comments! But our spiritual maturity grows when we resist returning evil for evil or anger for anger.

This social media storm did not need to upset my morning. I considered making a rational response but, knowing that he was unlikely to be persuaded by the logic and factual basis of my position, I bid him adieu and went on with my day. I sought to make an altar of the rubble of personal attack. I turned to calm and praise rather than anxiety and censure.

Singing our faith can transform our lives and change our attitudes, giving us courage and enabling us to become prophetic healers rather than angry ranters. I think of the freedom marchers singing "We Shall Overcome," while being bullied and battered by Southern law-enforcement officers. I imagine Martin Luther penning "A Mighty Fortress Is Our God" to confront his own personal depression. I remember the days after my only child was diagnosed with a life-threatening cancer, when the only chant I could stammer was, "Lord have mercy upon me, Christ have mercy upon me, Lord have mercy upon me." Then, as treatment began and hope emerged in the uncertainty, I discovered a hymn I learned as a child in the Baptist church:

> **Use whatever life brings you . . . as an opportunity to practice surrender. When you do, your pain will be anointed and filled with peace.**
>
> (Brother Lawrence)

Great is Thy faithfulness, O God my Father;
There is no shadow of turning with Thee,
Thou changest not, Thy compassions they fail not,
As Thou hast been, Thou forever wilt be.
Great is Thy faithfulness!
Great is Thy faithfulness!
Morning by morning new mercies I see
All I have needed Thy hand hath provided
Great is Thy faithfulness, Lord unto me!
Summer and winter and springtime and harvest,
Sun, moon, and stars in their courses above;
Join with all nature in manifold witness,
To Thy great faithfulness, mercy, and love.
Pardon for sin and a peace that endureth,
Thine own dear presence to cheer and to guide;
Strength for today, and bright hope for tomorrow
Blessings all mine, with ten thousand beside.

This hymn I learned in my childhood encompassed my pain and hope and still uplifts my spirits as I see my son, now married and the parent of two young boys, and know that in all the changes of life, nothing can separate us from the love of

It only takes a few short words, repeated throughout the day. "Make me according to Your heart, God. Make my thoughts Yours." And then the God of love rests in the depth and center of my soul. I cannot doubt that God is always there, at the very deepest level of my being.

(Brother Lawrence)

God. Great is God's faithfulness. All I have need of God's hand has provided. Singing my faith turned my heart from fear to praise, and despair to hope.

Each week, I tutor second graders in reading skills, and recently we came upon the word "praise." None of them were aware of its meaning—but they were delighted when I demonstrated it with words of approval and affirmation: "You're a really good reader," "I really like the way you corrected yourself on that word," "You're smart and can do good things." Like Brother Lawrence, I learned that when we live in a world of praise in which the heavens declare the glory of God and so do our cells, immune system, and words, I can see something holy—something amazing—hidden in those persons who make the most dubious or derisive posts. Unknown, perhaps even to themselves, the very process of posting, the intricacy of mind, body, and spirit, is worthy of affirmation and praise, even as I challenge their viewpoint.

Brother Lawrence recognized the importance of continuous communication with God. Every word can be a prayer, when it is dedicated to God. Every encounter can be an altar reminding us we are on holy ground. Dedicating each word to God shapes my encounters, whether in person or on social

> **God makes no great demands of us—simply remember God from time to time. . . . Lift up your heart to God, while you are eating, while you are talking with others. God will use the briefest moment.**
>
> *(Brother Lawrence)*

media. Brother Lawrence treated the people he served in the monastery kitchen as angels, that is, messengers of God. Perhaps the mystic remembered the words of Hebrews 13:2: "Do not neglect to show hospitality to strangers, for by this some have entertained angels without knowing it" (NASB).

Imagine that—hospitality on social media, angels on Facebook and Twitter! Yet deep down, if we believe the affirmation "God in all things, all things in God," then we must look for the angelic in the other and seek to bring forth the hidden angels, disguised by their incivility and ranting. Behold, hidden beneath a divisive and condescending post, a child of God dwells. Behold, hidden in a politician's tweet or a derisive social media post, a restless and troubled heart is unconsciously seeking God. As the Quakers assert, there is something of God in everyone. Our calling is to communicate from the Christ within us to the Christ within others. In the intricate interdependence of life, so evident in social media, we can choose to greet every person whose posts we see with the greeting Namaste, "I honor the Divine in you," or "the Christ in me greets the Christ in you." As the "better angels of our nature" emerge, to quote Abraham Lincoln, we may in some modest, yet meaningful way coax the "better angels" of others to come forth. In practicing the presence of God in our interactions and in our postings, we enable our own Divinity to burst forth, as we discover ourselves to be God's messengers—which is the literal meaning of angels—of healing and reconciliation. How can we keep from singing?

FINDING GOD ON THE INTERNET
God Talk on Social Media

Brother Lawrence sought to be in continuous conversation with God in the spirit of the apostle Paul who advised members of the Thessalonian congregation to deepen their spiritual lives through the following spiritual practice:

> *Rejoice always; pray without ceasing; in everything give thanks; for this is God's will for you in Christ Jesus. Do not quench the Spirit.* (I Thessalonians 5:16–19 NASB)

God is faithful, constantly moving in and through our lives. Still, we need to listen and respond to God. Our positive actions open the door for a greater influx of God's inspiration and energy. Prayer involves listening to the still, small voice of God speaking in our hearts in sighs too deep for words; it also involves an attitude of mind reflected in our attitudes, thoughts, and words, the words of our mouths and the meditations of our hearts.

What we say and how we say it matters. If we seek to speak the truth in love, then we must be particularly mindful of the words we use. Do our words reflect our personal conversations with God? Do they have the intention of helping rather than harming, and joining rather than separating? While we cannot ensure the quality of others' response, we can let God's words, grounded in continuous conversation with the Holy One, shape our words and responses, especially toward those with whom we disagree.

In this spiritual practice, let the spirit of Brother Lawrence and the apostle Paul guide you. As you sign on to social media or your Internet server, take a moment for the following spiritual practice:

- Quiet centering, breathing deeply God's presence and letting it fill you, body, mind, and spirit.
- Affirmation in the spirit of gratitude: "This is the day that God has made. I will rejoice and be glad in it."
- A brief prayer, such as, "Let me experience you, O God, in every communication. Let your words guide my words, so that whatever I say brings truth and healing to the world."
- Slow fingers: before you press "send," pause and examine your communication to see if it reflects your conversations with God.

In practicing God's presence on the Internet and social media, we create altars of healing and mindfulness that transform our lives and contribute a sense of calm to those around us. We may lower the emotional temperature in our Internet communities so we can discover common ground or agree to disagree without acrimony. Let us live our days in the spirit of the following prayer.

Prayer of Awareness and Transformation

Holy One, let me be in constant conversation with you, listening and sharing my joys and struggles, successes and disappointments. Let me practice your presence in every encounter. Let my communications be in synch with your Living Word moving through my mind, heart, and fingers. Let me be an instrument of peace. Amen.

Three

LISTENING TO YOUR LIFE

Frederick Buechner

"Go out and stand before me on the mountain," the Lord told him. And as Elijah stood there, the Lord passed by, and a mighty windstorm hit the mountain. It was such a terrible blast that the rocks were torn loose, but the Lord was not in the wind. After the wind there was an earthquake, but the Lord was not in the earthquake. And after the earthquake there was a fire, but the Lord was not in the fire. And after the fire there was the sound of a gentle whisper. When Elijah heard it, he wrapped his face in his cloak and went out and stood at the entrance of the cave. And a voice said, "What are you doing here, Elijah?"

(1 Kings 19:11-13 NLT)

It is precisely into the nonsense of our days that God speaks to us words of great significance—not words that are written in the stars but words that are written into the raw stuff and nonsense of our days, which are not nonsense just because God speaks into the midst of them. And the words that he says, to each of us differently, are: be brave...be merciful... feed my lambs...press on toward the goal.[6]

(Frederick Buechner)

Listen to your life, counsels author and theologian Frederick Buechner. In his memoir, entitled *Now and*

Then, Buechner says that this form of listening is the true essence and legacy of his writings:

> If I were called upon to state in a few words the essence of everything I was trying to say both as a novelist and as a preacher it would be something like this: Listen to your life. See it for the fathomless mystery that it is. In the boredom and pain of it no less than in the excitement and gladness: touch, taste, smell your way to the holy and hidden heart of it because in the last analysis all moments are key moments, and life itself is grace.[7]

Speaking of Buechner, editor Dale Brown writes:

God is right here in the thick of our day-by-day lives . . . trying to get messages through our blindness as we move around down here knee-deep in the fragrant muck and misery and marvel of the world. [Buechner's] work embodies "the persistent presentiment that Something is trying to get through in the midst of the muddle of our day-to-day lives."[8]

Cape Cod poet Mary Oliver asks, "What is it that you plan to do with your one wild and precious life?"[9] The foundation of wisdom is grounded in Socrates' counsel, "Know thyself," reflected in the multifaceted question with which he

> **The place God calls you to is the place where your deep gladness and the world's deep hunger meet.**
>
> *(Frederick Buechner)*

confronts the young Athenian Phaedrus: "Where have you come from and where are you going?"

Have you ever experienced a day in which you went from one activity to another and then upon going to bed ask yourself, "What happened today? Did I sleepwalk through it?" On such days of mindless activity we are convicted by the words of one of Mary Oliver's poems, which remind us that when we die, we don't want to regret being an observer and not an artist of our own lives.[10] Know who you are so that you have a heart of wisdom, recognizing the fragility and brevity of life and yet rejoicing in this wondrous and unrepeatable day. Such knowledge emerges in the interplay of private reflection, known only to you and God, and public participation, sharing from the deep wisdom flowing from your experience.

> **Pay attention to the things that bring a tear to your eye or a lump in your throat because they are signs that the holy is drawing near.**
>
> (Frederick Buechner)

This morning as I walked along Craigville Beach, I encountered a fellow walker, swinging her arms to the beat of a tune on her iPhone. I waved at her and boomed a "hello," but she didn't appear to notice me despite the fact I was just a few feet from her and walking in her direction. I wondered if she could hear her own heart speaking above the noise of her phone.

Listening to your life is not about siloed self-absorption, focusing only on your own experience, your circle of friends, and the political perspectives with which you agree. Self-absorption narrows our experience, cramping our spirits when their desire is to soar freely. There are times when we need to take out our ear buds and listen to the harmony of the spheres.

The life worth listening to is not just our unique experience but our lives in their fullness as they are connected to the whole universe. Each of us is a unique center of experience, emerging from and encompassed by Divinity, as the mystics report. We are also part of a lively universe of other centers of experience, permeated and energized by the Infinite God "whose center is everywhere and whose circumference is nowhere."[11] There are times when we need to focus, and block out environmental and interpersonal distractions—for example, when we are trying to complete a project or going on a solitary retreat—but even our solitude is connected with God and the dynamic universe flowing in and through us. The sheer silence, the still small voice, as Elijah experienced, cannot be separated from the wind, fire, and earthquake. There are times when we need to pray with our eyes—and our senses—wide open. The Spirit that groans in all creation also groans in us (Romans 8:22), and we need to let ourselves join focus with spacious attention to the graceful—sometimes disturbing—interdependence of life. Listening to your life means listening to the world around you and your own experience in all its mystery and chaos.

One of my graduate school professors Bernard Loomer describes the spiritual journey in terms of size or stature:

> By size I mean the stature of a person's soul, the range and depth of his love, his capacity for relationships. I mean the volume of life you can take into your being and still maintain your integrity and individuality, the intensity and variety of outlook you can entertain in the unity of

your being without feeling defensive or insecure. I mean the strength of your spirit to encourage others to become freer in the development of their diversity and uniqueness.[12]

The Gospel proclaims that "Jesus increased in wisdom and stature, and in favor with God and with people" (Luke 2:52 HCSB). Our calling in life and on the Internet is to be large-souled persons, who are in touch with their experience and empathetic with the experiences of others. The deeper our awareness of ourselves is, the more deeply we understand our connection with others and appreciate the burdens that each person carries.

What do you experience when you listen to your life? How does your life story shape your interactions on social media and the Internet? Our lives are a tapestry of experiences and encounters, coming together as the creative synthesis of each moment of experience.

> **Compassion is . . . the knowledge that there can never really be any peace and joy for me until there is peace and joy finally for you too.**
>
> *(Frederick Buechner)*

The philosopher Alfred North Whitehead asserts that the whole universe conspires to create each moment of experience. Our lives are not self-created or independent. They emerge from our responses to our past, family of origin, physical condition, gender, sexuality, economic status, and variety of other factors. We are creators, but our artistry emerges from the colors and words which we brush upon the canvas of our lives. In the biblical tradition, the most pitied person is the isolated, self-made person. Like the rich farmer, whose spiritual focus went no further than his individual largesse, we can gain the world and lose our souls (Luke 12:16–21).

I invite you to listen to your emotional life as you sign onto Facebook or Twitter. When I sign on to social media, I know in advance that some posts will irritate me and tempt me to respond in kind, letting my lesser angels run free. As an antidote to reptilian or combative responses, I breathe deeply to center myself and then note the images, feelings, and memories that arise as I read posts that anger, trouble, or attract me.

> **Words spoken in deep love or deep hate set things in motion in the human heart that can never be reversed.**
>
> *(Frederick Buechner)*

My spiritual counsel to my social media companions is this: When you find yourself upset at a post, pause to consider—What's pushing my buttons here? Why do I need to be right in this situation? What's inspiring my need to digitally demean a Facebook friend? What would it be like to be a Mahatma or Little Christ, big-spirited enough to embrace diversity without losing our spiritual centeredness?

In my own self-examination, I discover that I am often upset at another person for reasons that are unrelated to their words and actions or that my irritation is related to how well I know the person. Are they merely objects with which to contend or do I have a personal history that allows me to respond person-to-person civilly and respectfully? If I can move my perspective closer to the person in question, so that I see him or her as someone real and nuanced, it becomes harder to scornfully dismiss this individual.

We are mysteries to ourselves, but as we mine the depths of our own experiences, we discover our connection with others, including those who push all our buttons, whether in a church meeting, on the drive home, or on the Internet. Our own spiritual archeological quests may surface painful strata, but in the deep mystery of ourselves, we may discover an even deeper Mystery, the Holy Adventure flowing uniquely through our lives and actions toward the world around us. For those who listen, life will never be boring or uninteresting. "In the midst of the muddle of our day-to-day lives," each day will bring new revelations. We will discover the wonder of all creation flowing through us and everyone we meet.

> **Wherever people love each other and are true to each other and take risks for each other, God is with them and for them and they are doing God's will.**
>
> *(Frederick Buechner)*

FINDING GOD ON THE INTERNET
Listening to Your Life

Over three decades ago, I learned a chant at Washington, DC's Shalem Institute for Spiritual Formation: "I thank you God for the wonder of my being." This affirmation is at the heart of the process of listening to your life. You are, as God's beloved child, a unique and dynamic embodiment of the Holy One, with unique experiences, emotions, challenges, hopes, and dreams. Your life is interesting and full of possibilities.

Moreover, we are all partly mysteries to ourselves, never fully aware of the forces at work in our unconscious, life history, or physical-spiritual-intellectual being. Nor are we fully aware of God's movements in our lives. Life is a constant process of self-discovery in which we and God are new every morning.

This exercise is twofold. Over the coming week, take ten to fifteen minutes each day to explore the "wonder of your being" and the "fathomless mystery of your life." Begin this process with a time of silence, followed by the affirmation, "I thank you God for the wonder of my being." After a few minutes, pause to notice how you are feeling in the present moment (joyful, apprehensive, anxious, adventurous, curious, angry, loving, and so forth). What images, inclinations, and ideas are shaping your life at this moment? How are they connected with your past experiences? How might they lead into future adventures? What creative sparks are emerging in this very moment? What possibilities are being born in the womb of your experience?

Then, looking at the big picture, what would it be like to have the spiritual stature to welcome diversity, challenge injustice and falsehood, and maintain your spiritual integrity, while bathing those with whom you disagree with God's love?

Take a few minutes to journal your experience as a way of preserving this fleeting moment and deepening your experience. Conclude by giving thanks for "the wonder of your being" and asking God to remind you throughout the day of your unique experience and perspective on the world.

The second half of this spiritual exercise involves practicing "the wonder of your being" on social media. An alternative version of the Shalem chant is "I thank you God for the wonder of *all* being." Gratitude grounds us in the intricate interdependence of life, connects us with the wellsprings of Divine providence moving through our lives, and inspires us to do something beautiful for God as our contribution to the world beyond our present time and place. Meister Eckhardt once said that "if the only prayer you can say in your life is thank you, that will be enough." As you sign on to social media or the Internet, make this affirmation: "I thank you God for the wonder of my being. I thank you God for the wonder of all being. I thank you God for my social media companions in the wonder of their being."

The wonder of your being calls you to aim for the highest and best in all your interactions. It challenges you never to diminish the unique manifestation of Divinity that constitutes your life or another's. Aim high in your communications. The "wonder of all being" awakens us to the unique manifestation of Divinity in everything else, including the Facebook friend who claims climate change is a hoax or who proudly displays a meme that you discover, upon research, is patently false; the person who has tried to refute your viewpoint by name-calling; the high-school classmate who appears to think a politician you find despicable is the second person of the Trinity, worthy of adoration and praise for his insight into every political issue; and the outspoken critic who castigates you for considering other perspectives on issues such as abortion, universal health care, or the environment. Like the grasshopper in Mary Oliver's poem "The Summer Day," every person is more than meets the eye. Each is amazing and unique, manifesting the wonder of all being.

As Buechner reminds us, we are called to pay attention. To see the wonder of another's being and your own inspires us to civility and humanity as we challenge others' positions, not with cheap shots or name-calling, but with respect, factual statements, and carefully thought-out theological or spiritual arguments.

In listening to your life, let the unfathomable mystery come to the surface, noting your reactions to certain statements as well as moments of self-transcendence. Let your holiness shine through prayerfully awakening to the holiness in others.

Prayer of Awareness and Transformation

I thank you God for the wonder of my being, the fathomless mystery of who I am and who you are. I thank you for the wonder of all being and your presence hidden and revealed in every face. Remind today to truly pay attention, that I may see my life as holy and my path as holy ground. Bless my thoughts as I communicate and my fingers as I type that I might bring beauty, truth, goodness, and holiness into the world, playing my part in healing the world one keystroke at a time. Amen.

Four

DAILY ATTENTIVENESS

Ignatius of Loyola

Besides this, you know what time it is, how it is now the moment for you to wake from sleep. For salvation is nearer to us now than when we became believers; the night is far gone, the day is near. Let us then lay aside the works of darkness and put on the armor of light; let us live honorably as in the day, not in reveling and drunkenness, not in debauchery and licentiousness, not in quarreling and jealousy. Instead, put on the Lord Jesus Christ, and make no provision for the flesh, to gratify its desires.

(Romans 13:11–14)

Jesus, may all that is you flow into me. . . . Let me not run from the love you offer. But hold me safe from the forces of evil. On each of my dyings shed your light and love. Keep calling to me until that day comes, when, with your saints, I may praise you forever.[13]

What I want above all is the ability to respond freely to God, and all other loves for people, places, and things are held in proper perspective by the light and strength of God's grace.

(Ignatius of Loyola)

"There's a war out there!" So, say the social media and political pundits. A war of words and incivility in which, in the words of Coach Vince Lombardi, "Winning isn't everything. It's the only thing!" Such mottos are a far cry from what I learned as boy playing Little League baseball: "It's not whether you win or lose, it's how you play the game."

Politics and social media have promoted the scorched-earth policy of communication. Such binary win-lose approaches to faith and politics have led religious leaders to overlook truth and ethics and excused governmental traumatizing of children at our borderlands or political misconduct in order to gain political power. Many of us have deactivated our spiritual GPS to gain the upper hand in arguments, bullying and dehumanizing our opponents, name-calling and dismissing positions with which we differ.

There appear to be two contrasting and competing moral and political universes, unable to find common ground, each claiming to be right, while the opponent is clearly wrong. While I believe that there are definite gradations of maturity, fact, and spiritual and political insight, and I stand by own spiritual and political values as reflective of the hard work of contemplation, research, biblical studies, and factfinding, I recognize that when we succumb to binary divisions of light and darkness, truth and error, our victory is Pyrrhic. In the process of winning we may lose our souls.

> **He who goes about to reform the world must begin with himself, or he loses his labor.**
>
> *(Ignatius of Loyola)*

We have drifted from the abundant spiritual life which God wants for us.

There is also a spiritual battle going on inside us. The apostle Paul describes our inner turmoil: "I do not understand my own actions. For I do not do what I want, but I do the very thing I hate" (Romans 7:15). Each moment we are presented with the choice: to turn toward love or hate, truth or falsehood, hospitality or alienation. We struggle to follow the better angels of our nature, knowing that when we fight fire with fire, we may destroy the things we hold most dear, our compassion and integrity.

Once again, this morning, like many other mornings, I struggled to follow the better angels of my nature. As usual, one of my social media friends posted a blatant lie, easily documented, about a political leader I respect. I've done my research on the issue he raised and am convinced of the factuality and integrity of my position. I felt a spasm of anger, and wanted to set my social media friend straight, outlining his stupidity and intolerance with a one-liner of my own. I wrote the post. It was clever and incisive and would surely alert him to the error of his ways and point him toward the truth. And then I paused. I was reacting, not creating. Even if I was factually correct and stood on the moral

> **No idle word should be uttered. I understand a word to be idle when it serves no good purpose, either for myself or for another, and was not intended to do so.**
>
> *(Ignatius of Loyola)*

high ground, insult would lead to injury, further alienation, and a diminishment of my own spiritual status. For a moment, his words had taken control of my spirit, eliciting an angry reaction, when what is most important is that I respond out of freedom, truth, and love. Liberated from my own version of Pavlov's response, I savored my post and then deleted it. I surrounded my friend in God's light, asking that both of us be illumined by God's presence in our lives. I chose to exercise my freedom by not taking the bait!

The philosopher William James believed the primary battlegrounds of life are spiritual and moral rather than military in nature. Ignatius of Loyola (1491–1556), the founder of the Society of Jesus, the Jesuits, embodied this concept, placing spiritual and moral obedience as far higher priorities than any military victory. He did not start out his life with this understanding, however.

Enamored by war and personal honor, Ignatius entered the military and rose to prominence in the court of the Duke of Najera. Fighting on the behalf of the Duke, Ignatius was gravely injured when a cannonball ricocheted off a wall, striking his leg and leaving him temporarily crippled. Forced to return to his father's home in Loyola, the recuperating Ignatius wanted to plunge himself into reading romance novels that celebrated chivalrous behaviors. When he found these novels in short supply, he turned to books on the lives of Jesus and the saints and discovered a vastly different form of heroism in a life devoted to serving God.

One of the texts that shaped Ignatius's spiritual path, written by Ludoph of Saxony, invited readers to imaginatively enter the Gospels' stories as observers or participants. This technique of simple contemplative prayer eventually evolved into Ignatius's Spiritual Exercises. Fully recovered, yet from then on walking with a limp, Ignatius devoted himself to Christ as his Lord and Sovereign. He became a pilgrim and eventually gathered the nucleus of followers whose commitment would give birth to the Society of Jesus.

At the heart of Ignatius's vision of reality was the affirmation that scripture as God's revelation invites us to become contemporaries with its stories, encountering scripture with all our senses as well as our imagination. The Bible is living word, animating the present moment, challenging us to choose between life and death, and light and darkness, in our relationships and spiritual journeys. In scripture, God addresses us in the now, calling us to follow, embodying God's mission in the world in the same spirit as a soldier following a superior officer.

> **Whatever you are doing, that which makes you feel the most alive . . . that is where God is.**
>
> *(Ignatius of Loyola)*

To face the inner and outer challenges of life we need to put on the whole armor of God:

> Therefore take up the whole armor of God, so that you may be able to withstand on that evil day, and having done everything, to stand firm. Stand therefore, and fasten the belt of truth around your waist, and put on the breastplate of righteousness. As shoes for your feet put on whatever will make you ready to proclaim the gospel

of peace. With all of these, take the shield of faith, with which you will be able to quench all the flaming arrows of the evil one. Take the helmet of salvation, and the sword of the Spirit, which is the word of God. Pray in the Spirit at all times in every prayer and supplication. To that end keep alert and always persevere in supplication for all the saints. (Ephesians 6:13–18)

Recognizing that we are surrounded by God's protection and that nothing can separate us from the love of God, we discover that others' posts can't threaten us, nor do they need to ensnare us in controversy (Romans 8:38–39). We are in God's hands regardless of what emerges in our daily lives and in social media. God's armor of light surrounds us and illumines us as we navigate the minefields of social media communication.

Though nearly two thousand years separate us from Jesus' earthly ministry and the completion of the biblical canon, we can discover our vocation by imaginatively placing ourselves in biblical passages, visualizing the environment, actors, responses to God, and our own presence in responding to God's call. In a similar way, we can read Facebook posts as sources of insight and revelation, even those which we perceive as off the mark, knowing that all of us are part of God's moral arc, the providential movements of grace that lure us toward God's Shalom. Seeing ourselves as part of a Divine drama, in which we have an important role, we can ask God to enlighten us in

People who carry God in their heart bear Heaven with them wherever they go.

(Ignatius of Loyola)

our responses to falsehoods as well as in open sharing of our own truth.

Ignatius encouraged his followers to practice prayer-filled mindfulness by following the discipline of what he called the Daily Examen. The Examen is a technique of prayerful reflection on the events of the day in order to detect God's presence and to discern Divine direction for us. Although formulated more than four hundred years ago, the Examen is as practical today as it has ever been. It is a useful spiritual tool for our online lives as well, proving that just as God called to our parents in faith in many and diverse ways, God still calls us today. Spiritual practice does not go out of date, for God is still speaking!

FINDING GOD ON THE INTERNET
Social Media Examen

Often when a companion asks, "How are you?" I often give a perfunctory response, such as, "I'm ok," or, "Just fine," regardless of how I am currently feeling. In that passing moment, I don't want to take the time to share my current life situation or state of mind—or frankly, I really don't know how I'm feeling.

In my role as a pastor and spiritual guide, I often address persons facing serious illness with a similar but deeper question "How are things with your soul?" The results are often as revealing as surprising. The question invites both inquisitor and respondent to consider the quality of their relationship to God, their deepest motivations, shortcomings, and successes, and—as one of my Jesuit spiritual directors noted—moments of consolation and desolation, intimacy and distance from God. Such soulful reflection is at the heart of the Examen, a process which is typically done at the end of the day or can be done upon rising or several times throughout the day as a way of taking notice and then calibrating your spiritual GPS.

Examination of Conscience

Ignatius suggests the following in relationship to the Examination of Conscience: "It is often found helpful to set aside about midway in the day and again at the end of the day before retiring in a formal review of how I have spent the day," not primarily as a confession of sin but as "a way to integrate my day, more wholly fixing it on God."

These are the basic elements of Ignatius's approach to the Examen:

1. Giving thanks to God for all that I have received.
2. Asking the Holy Spirit to enlighten me so that I see my shortcomings, or sins, from God's perspective.
3. Going over the events of the day in terms of times of where I have failed to follow God's way by commission or omission in thought word and deed.
4. Expressing sorrow and asking for God's healing forgiveness.
5. Praying for God's strength to amend my life.[14]

Most twenty-first-century persons will do their Examen on the fly, shoehorning it amid the demands of their busy schedules. Few of us take weeklong retreats, and we may have just a few minutes at lunch time or after putting our children or grandchildren to bed or returning from a social engagement. A twenty-first-century version of the Examen might be limited to five to ten minutes of silence and reflection such as the following:

1. A time of silence, breathing deeply God's presence in your life for a few moments, feeling a sense of God's movements in every moment of life.

2. A moment of thanksgiving for the God-moments and graces of the day.

3. A prayer that the Holy Spirit reveal moments of faithfulness and inattentiveness, blessing and alienation throughout the day.

4. A moment of review of my Internet and social media communications in light of God's calling to wholeness.

5. Prayer of confession, placing my faithfulness and imperfection in God's care, and asking God to guide me toward wholeness in thought, word, and deed.

6. Opening to God's sustaining love to overcome my temptations to alienation and God-forgetfulness in daily actions and on the Internet and social media.

Placing our whole selves before God in prayer heals our sense of defensiveness and inadequacy and enables us to face social media conflicts, knowing that God's light surrounds and protects us.

Visualizing God's Presence Online

Ignatius believed that it is important for us to "enter into the vision of God," aligning ourselves with God's experience of the world in its joy and sorrow, to try to blend God's perspective and our own in understanding scripture as well as the events of our lives.

In describing his approach to the Annunciation of Mary (Luke 1:26–38), Ignatius invites us to "stay with the eyes of God, and look upon the young girl Mary, as she is greeted by God. I let myself be wholly present to the scene, hearing the nuances of the questions, seeing the expression in the face and eyes, watching the gestures and the movements which tell us so much about a person." In a similar way, we can respond to a scripture with our whole person, body, mind, spirit, senses, imagination, putting ourselves in the scene, from a God's-eye view or from the point of view of a participant or the key figure of the biblical passage.

This same process of visualization can be used to explore an Internet encounter in the course of your day. Looking back at a social media interaction, for example, you can visualize God's presence guiding you and the people with whom you are positively or negatively communicating, enabling you to intuit their joys and sorrows, fears and hopes. You can prayerfully look at your own response, exploring from a wider perspective your own interactions as they added to or subtracted from the holiness of the moment. You might imagine yourself choosing another path of communication and care. You can visualize yourself following your better angels in your response or your choice to abstain from responding. In that spirit, you might see yourself in a friendly conversation with your social media companions, learning about them as you share your viewpoint with a loving heart. We cannot totally undo the past, but with prayerful, creative imagination, we can lay the foundation for a holier, more whole future. What's more, as you enter into this, you will gain practice at listening for God's guidance in your Internet interactions, luring you toward more healing responses.

Prayer of Awareness and Transformation

Holy and Loving God, I bring my whole self to you, asking you to bless my interactions and encounters. Challenge me to see you as my intimate companion in every interaction and encounter. Guide me to the path of wholeness of love that my social media conversations might become sanctuaries of grace, motivated by your quest for Shalom. Amen.

Five

PEACE IS EVERY POST

Thich Nhat Hanh

Peace I leave with you;
my peace I give to you.
I do not give to you as the world gives.
Do not let your hearts be troubled,
and do not let them be afraid.

(John 14:27)

Every morning, when we wake up,
we have twenty-four
brand-new hours to live.

**What a precious gift!
We have the capacity to live in a way
that these twenty-four hours will bring
peace, joy, and happiness
to ourselves and others.**[15]

**Before making a phone call,
you can also breathe in and
breathe out three times,
then dial.**

(Thich Nhat Hanh)

The Internet and social media are anything but peaceful these days. Otherwise courteous and good-hearted people log on to social media and fall under the spell of incivility, invective, and name-calling. People who prize the facts in their daily lives and pride themselves on their honesty and community involvement post patently false memes and dismiss opposing positions, without presenting an argument, with terms such as "fascist," "libtard," "racist," "sexist," or "snowflake," and these are the polite terms. Many of us abandon truth, rationality, and compassion the moment we sign on to our social media accounts.

Social scientists suggest many reasons for the growing incivility: culture wars, media polarization, stress, rapid change and future shock, political manipulation, xenophobia, inability to adapt to explosion of information, and uncertainty about our personal, national, and global futures. Unlike previous eras when communication was primarily face to face or voice to voice, the virtual nature of communication allows us to communicate regularly with people we barely know and whose joys and sorrows are a mystery to us. Social media creates threads of often contentious dialogue among people who have never met. We make assumptions about one another's characters and values based on 280 characters in a tweet or a paragraph or meme on a Facebook post. We vent our anger and rage, thinking ourselves to be responding to cardboard characters and not living, breathing humans, knowing they have no recourse but to respond in kind. And, so it goes, with greater alienation one post at a time! Rather than bringing us together, our communication has led to polarization and objectification. We are known by our social media posts and not our inner lives. We are known by our differences, not the essential unity we share.

> **When you begin to see that your enemy is suffering, that is the beginning of insight.**
>
> *(Thich Nhat Hanh)*

As I've noted throughout this text, I am often tempted to follow the voices of rebuke rather than healing. On occasion, I succumb to agitation on social media when I view what I perceive as the falsehoods and incivility of others. My initial response to many of the posts I view is intellectual disbelief:

I can't imagine such blatant, or unconscious, ignorance or prevarication. Then, I realize that I am spiraling into letting other people determine my state of mind and emotional life. I need to take a breath, begin again, and find my spiritual center.

For many people, the master of peaceful breathing in times of stress is the Vietnamese Buddhist monk, Thich Nhat Hanh, or "Teacher on One Action" (born 1926). Thich Nhat Hanh, affectionately known as "Thay," entered the monastic life at age twelve, but like Thomas Merton, he recognized that his spiritual commitments required him to become a social activist. In his quest for peace, Thich Nhat Hanh refused to take sides between the warring Vietnamese factions, leading to accusations of treason and eventual exile. His vision of "engaged Buddhism" joined contemplation with political activism in the quest for the common good. Thay realized that in the middle of conflict, we can be peace crusaders and peaceful too. We can be advocates for our causes and see the humanity of those whose policies we challenge.

> **Each thought, each action in the sunlight of awareness becomes sacred.**
>
> (Thich Nhat Hanh)

Whether we are contemplatives, activists, or a hybrid, we can start our days with the quest for peace amid the storm. Thich Nhat Hanh counsels:

> Peace is present right here, in ourselves and everything we do and see. The question is whether or not we are in touch with it.

The choice for peace is made moment by moment. As A.J. Muste averred, "There is no way to peace. Peace is the way."[16]

I have found great wisdom in Thich Nhat Hanh's phone meditation: "Before making a phone call, you can also breathe in and breathe out three times, then dial." If you're old enough—and I am—you probably remember "dial up" Internet. You logged on and heard the ringing until you made contact. In the days before high-speed Internet, getting on the Internet took as long as a minute, and I would grow impatient. As an antidote to my own impatience, I established a regular contemplative practice that I still follow: I take a few deep breaths, reestablishing my sense of spiritual equanimity. I discovered that nuisances and inconveniences can be a source of spiritual growth. Can the same be true of people who push our buttons? Can their behaviors be an invitation to peace-making?

> **No blame, no reasoning, no argument, just understanding. If you understand, and you show that you understand, you can love, and the situation will change.**
>
> *(Thich Nhat Hanh)*

These days, high-speed Internet is so quick that I'm on the Internet or the social media site almost before I can inhale! Still, I have found Thich Nhat Hanh's practice helpful in grounding myself in God and not allowing the passing news feed or social media comment to determine my spiritual temperature. Thich Nhat Hanh counsels this brief breath meditation similar in approach to the phone meditation:

Breathing in, I calm my body.
Breathing out, I smile.
Dwelling in the present moment,
I know this is a wonderful moment.

In this time of high-speed Internet, I often pause before I sign on with a variation of Thich Nhat Hanh's phone prayer:

Breathing in, I calm my body, mind, and spirit.
Breathing out I sign in with joy and friendship.
Dwelling in this holy moment,
I awaken to gratitude and wonder.
I share Christ with every post.
In this wonderful moment, I am one with everyone online.

And, it is a wonderful moment! I woke up this morning with all its possibilities for adventure, blessing, and connecting. This is truly the day God has made. In waking up, I am filled with gratitude and wonder. How wonderful it is to be able to communicate with people across the globe, sharing goodness and beauty! This is the joy of what Thich Nhat Hanh describes as "interbeing." In Thay's words, "The truth is that everything is everything else. We can only inter-be, not just be. And we are responsible for everything that happens to us. . . . We are not separated. We are inextricably inter-related. The rose is the garbage, and the non-prostitute is the prostitute. The rich man is the poor woman, and the Buddhist is the non-Buddhist."[17] The unity envisaged by the creators of the World Wide Web, and touted by today's Facebook commercials is our deepest reality, and I can witness to this unity with every post.

I can protest presidential malpractice and challenge climate denial with grace rather than violence.

Thich Nhat Hanh's poem from *Peace Is Every Step*, "Call Me By My True Names," captures the essence of living gracefully amid the tragic beauty of our world. After itemizing the ways that we are all one—both victim and violator—he concludes with the call to "wake up," so that "the door of my heart can be left open, the door of compassion." In an interdependent world, we mirror one another. There is no "other," nor is anyone alien to me As we open the door of compassion, we discover that we are all Buddhas and Christs in training, and we are all mystics in the making. Inspired by Thich Nhat Hanh's poem, I realize:

> **Mindfulness must be engaged. Once there is seeing, there must be acting. Otherwise, what's the use of seeing?**
>
> *(Thich Nhat Hanh)*

I am the angry white supremacist in Charlottesville.

I am teenage Greta Thunberg protesting climate denial.

I am the beer-bellied Pennsylvanian with the red "Make America Great Again" hat.

I am the Parkland, Florida, teen, anxious about going to class.

I am the climate-change denier and the gun-rights enthusiast.

I am the transgendered person preparing for surgery.

I am the fundamentalist preacher, spouting hatred toward gays and lesbians.

I am the gay couple at their wedding ceremony.

I am the high school student who posts a misogynist meme.

I am the teenager considering suicide.

I am the national leader who lies incessantly for political gain.

I am the single parent going from paycheck to paycheck.

I am the billionaire taking his last breath and knowing he can't take it with him.

I am a Buddha in training and a little Christ filled with healing love!

"This is us": humankind in its wondrous and tragic diversity, as the television show asserts. We are all in this together, and by breathing in and out I can calm my spirit, recognize my unity with all creation, and become an agent of Divine healing and compassion. One breath at a time, we can become social-media Bodhisattvas, bringing peace to every interaction.

FINDING GOD ON THE INTERNET
Peace Is Every Breath

Thich Nhat Hanh invites us to spiritual self-awareness. In the spirit of mystics everywhere, he encourages us to view every moment as a window to Divinity. Every act can be enlightened or a doorway to enlightenment. As we mindfully breathe, walk, work, and share on social media, we can be guided by the wisdom of Gautama and the compassion of Jesus.

Take a Breath!

Mystics throughout the ages remind us that the simplest and most universal activities can be the source of the greatest spiritual insight. Breathing mindfully and slowly grounds and centers, reduces stress, and restores calm. Conscious breathing connects us with all creation in one great Divine Breath, indeed, the Spirit of God that Jesus bestowed on his disciples on Easter night (John 20:19–22).

There are many ways to breathe God's Spirit with mindfulness. In fact, every breath can be a prayer if we devote our breaths to God and our neighbor, whether at home, work, or on social media.

- Breathing and opening to insight when I log onto my computer, especially when it takes longer than I expect or when my Internet is unexpectedly disconnected.
- Breathing gently and deeply when I experience myself becoming stressed or busy while responding to professional e-mail communications.
- Breathing before I post a response on Facebook, especially one that elicits anger or anxiety.
- Breathing as I gaze at loved ones, a stranger, or the photo of a friend on Facebook.

Every breath can become a prayer for those who awaken to the everlasting and holy now in which we live and move and have our being. Thich Nhat Hanh advises us to use the following statement as we breath calmly and deeply:

> Breathing in, I calm my body.
> Breathing out, I smile.
> Dwelling in the present moment,
> I know this is a wonderful moment.

I regularly use a breath prayer I learned from Allan Armstrong Hunter during my graduate studies at Claremont Graduate School and Claremont School of Theology:

> I breathe the Spirit deeply in
> And blow it gently out again.

We Are One in the Spirit

Thich Nhat Hanh's poem, "Call Me by My True Names," describes the essential interdependence of life. There is no other. Every creature mirrors and touches me and inspires me to compassion.

Daily read the poem "Call Me by My True Names" and my companion thoughts as a prelude to signing onto the Internet or your social media account. Let these ideas inspire you to "radical amazement," described as the heart of religion by Rabbi Abraham Joshua Heschel. Experience your essential unity with everyone you observe on social media.

Be Mindful and Block

There are times when our feelings consistently get the best of us. We don't yet have the spiritual stature to maintain our equanimity when we read a Facebook companion's posts. We become angry and want to fight back. In such circumstances, you may ask the question: What am I getting out of this social media "friendship?" Is it causing more harm than good?

There are times when we simply need to absent ourselves from situations that threaten our emotional well-being until we have greater self-awareness. If certain social media companions push all your emotional buttons, say a prayer for them and then "block" them from your wall. You don't need to inflict what you perceive to be hatred or dishonesty on your personal account. You can choose peace by changing your environment while you are also trying to change your spiritual life. As you let go of a troublesome companion, you might breathe in God's wondrous peace.

Prayer of Awareness and Transformation

Breathe on me, breath of God. Fill me with life anew. Awaken me to the holiness of life, the wonder of each moment, and the unity I share with all creation. Let me bring joy and healing to every living being. Amen.

Six

DOING ORDINARY THINGS WITH GREAT LOVE

Therese of Lisieux

Jesus also said, "With what can we compare the kingdom of God, or what parable will we use for it? It is like a mustard seed, which, when sown upon the ground, is the smallest of all the seeds on earth; yet when it is sown it grows up and becomes the greatest of all shrubs, and puts forth large branches, so that the birds of the air can make nests in its shade."

(Mark 4:30–32)

When I am feeling nothing, when I am incapable of praying, of practicing virtue, then is the moment for seeking opportunities, nothings, which please Jesus more than mastery of the world or even martyrdom suffered with generosity. For example, a friendly word when I would like to say nothing, or put on a look of annoyance.[18]

(Therese of Lisieux)

Therese of Lisieux (1873–1897) lived a brief life, virtually unnoticed by the world, and not particularly notable even in her own monastic community. Shortly before her death, one of her fellow sisters noted: "My sister Therese of the Child of Jesus is going to die soon; and I really wonder what our mother [superior] is going to say after her death. She will be very embarrassed, for this little sister, as likeable as she is, has done nothing worth the trouble of being recounted."[19] Yet, despite her desire to be hidden in God, the "little way" of Therese led the Roman Catholic Church to canonize her as a saint in 1925. In 1997, Pope John Paul II declared her the thirty-third Doctor of the Church, the youngest person, and one of only four women so named (the others being Teresa of Ávila, Hildegard of Bingen, and Catherine of Siena). Therese recognized that God had given her no great work. Instead, she spread little flowers of love and kindness—what we call "random acts of kindness"—dedicated to Jesus. The world is saved one action at a time and ordinary actions, repeatedly done with love, transform the world.

Therese's "little way" embodied the spirit of an earlier Carmelite, Brother Lawrence, who counseled that authentic spirituality involves practicing the presence of God one simple act at a time. Love not notoriety makes the world go 'round.

Sister Marie of the Trinity described Therese's path with these words:

> **Love needs to be proved by action.**[20]
>
> *(Therese of Lisieux)*

> [she] has done nothing extraordinary: no ecstasies, no revelations, no mortification which frighten little souls like ours. Her whole life can be summed up in one word: she loved God in all the ordinary actions of common life, performing them with great faithfulness . . . not even to seek to keeping an account of whether you make [spiritual] progress or not. That's not our business. We have only to perform all the little acts of daily life with the greatest possible love, to recognize humbly, but without sadness, our thousand imperfections which are always resurfacing and to ask God with confidence to transform them into love.[21]

Therese shows us that every day can be chockful of gentle and undramatic encounters with God when we devote the common and quotidian acts of work, play, and home to

God. Ultimately, what Therese embodied is mindful activity, grounded in a moment-by-moment dedication of our lives to God's way of Shalom. Awareness that we are always on holy ground, that every moment can be a theophany, and that God's gentle providence moves through all things.

Each moment is a window into Divinity. Each encounter a "thin place," as the Celtic Christians say, where time and eternity meet, and the world becomes transparent to God. In that thin place, we see the wonder of ourselves and those around us. In the spirit of William Blake, the doors of perception are cleansed, and we see clearly infinity in a grain of sand, newborn baby—or our Facebook companions.

> **Our Lord does not look so much at the greatness of our actions, nor even at their difficulty, as at the love with which we do them.**
>
> *(Therese of Lisieux)*

Small can be beautiful. The domestic can be Divine. While my grandchildren delight in trips to Disneyworld and Universal Studios Harry Potter Land, these special moments are the frosting on the cake. Their sense of security and feelings of being loved emerge from simple acts of attentive care done day after day. Looking back on your lifetime, you seldom remember an ordinary day, and yet a lifetime of ordinary days, permeated with love, give a child a sense of worth and a moral compass.

A mustard seed grows into a great plant, providing shelter in the storms of life. Five loves and two fish feed a multitude. A small group of disciples, women and men, gathered in an upper room receive the blessings of the resurrected Jesus and become a great spiritual movement. In God's interdependent universe, any moment can be the catalyst for spiritual transformation.

Scientists recognize that small acts can lead to great outcomes. From a small drop of energy nearly fourteen billion years ago, the universe burst forth. A butterfly flapping its wings on a California beach can change the weather patterns on Cape Cod where I live. A small act of kindness, unnoticed even by the giver, can set in motion a chain of events that changes individuals and communities.

Ordinary actions, often unnoticed, bring healing and reconciliation to the world. This morning, a Facebook friend posted about her current health situation, describing the recurrence of a life-threatening illness. As I have done several times before, I "messaged" her privately, expressing my prayers and telling her that I will be giving her a distant reiki healing energy treatment later in the morning. She expressed her gratitude and later tells me that she's feeling much better and is strengthened to know that I am praying for her. Later that day, I reached out to another social media companion, still mourning the death of her companion animal. Her communication inspired me to call her a few days later, offering her my listening ear and sharing a few of the practices, aimed at calming the spirit, found in this text. Social media always gives us an opportunity to choose paths of love and communion rather

> **Each small task of everyday life is part of the total harmony of the universe.**
>
> *(Therese of Lisieux)*

than incivility and alienation. We can choose to listen to God speaking in the lives of others and then respond in the spirit of Jesus, doing good to the least of these.

Therese of Lisieux knew nothing of the Internet and social media. Electricity and the telephone may even have been novelties to her. Still, she has a message we need to hear as we live out our lives one post at a time: Do ordinary things with great love. Make your posts testimonies to God's grace. Spread flowers of kindness wherever you go and with everyone with whom you interact.

> **My vocation, at last I have found it; my vocation is love.**
>
> *(Therese of Lisieux)*

For many of us, the Internet and social media are truly ordinary. They have become as normal as breathing. We log on at the beginning of each day and take one last look before retiring for the night. They are central to our work lives and our recreation, and we are seldom apart from our cell phones and the myriad applications they can house.

Yesterday as I sat with a dozen parents, watching my grandson's soccer practice, every one of the parents was scrolling through their cell phones. They would look up from time to time to watch the scrimmage and then return to their online

> **Miss no single opportunity of making some small sacrifice, here by a smiling look, there by a kindly word; always doing the smallest right and doing it all for love.**
>
> *(Therese of Lisieux)*

activities. That's how ubiquitous the Internet is in our daily lives. Our use of social media and the Internet can be superficial, or it can awaken us to what Kathleen Norris describes as the "quotidian mysteries" of life. Every post we view is Beth-El, a gateway to God, and every post we make shapes the future of those with whom we interact and, dare we say, the world.

> To pick up a pin out of love can transform another's soul.
>
> (Therese of Lisieux)

Ordinary things done with great love! That's a tall order at any time. But how might we live this out in the context of social media incivility and fabrication? Can we speak the truth with love? Whenever we communicate, whether our words are prophetic, mundane, or perfunctory, can we live by the words of Hebrews 13:2: "Do not neglect to show hospitality to strangers, for by doing that some have entertained angels without knowing it"? I have begun to prayerfully ponder every post, asking if my posts come from a place of love or fear, friendship or anger, help or harm. Do I really seek to be loving regardless of the behaviors I witness online? I confess I'm always in process, and am tempted to lash out, but then Love intervenes, and I pause and pray, "God help me to do the loving thing in this response."

FINDING GOD ON THE INTERNET
Ordinary Posts with Great Love

Jewish mystics proclaim that when you save a soul, you save the world. Jesus' parable of the lost sheep suggests that the ninety-nine need the one as much as she needs them. Without the return of the lost one, the flock will be incomplete. Therese of Lisieux would go further to proclaim that the world is saved one action at a time. Faithfulness simply calls us to respond with love regardless of the outcome. Whether or not they are noticed, acts of kindness change us and those with whom we communicate. A word of consolation or praise can change a person's day. Our ordinary, moment-by-moment actions, play a role in *tikkun olam*—mending or saving the world. We plant the seeds of beauty and trust the harvest to God. As Therese believed, we can do small actions with great love—and that great love practiced every day saves us and the world.

In the spirit of Therese of Lisieux, make a commitment to doing ordinary things with great love. Choose love in every action on the Internet and social media. You may never notice the difference you make with a word of affirmation, reconciliation, or healthy challenge. Like George Bailey, protagonist of the film *It's a Wonderful Life*, however, we may discover that ordinary acts of generosity can bring healing to countless people and salvation to our communities.

One Prayer at a Time, One Post at a Time

Therese of Lisieux believed that conscious commitments to healing actions are undergirded by a life of prayer dedicated to Jesus and his vision. Therese invites us to live each day in an attitude of prayer. From her perspective, transformative prayer is the gift of attentiveness to God's gentle providence in every moment of our lives. Prayer is more than an occasional practice, quickly forgotten amid the welter of everyday activities. Prayer is the air we breathe, and every breath can become a prayer for those around us and to the One who gives us life and love. As Therese wrote, "Prayer is an aspiration of the heart, a simple glance directed to heaven, a cry of gratitude and love in the midst of trial as well as joy . . . expanding my soul and uniting me with Jesus."

As you sign on to your social media accounts, take a deep breath and affirm, "I do ordinary activities with great love." As you take deep breaths, visualize every post you will encounter on social media as an opportunity to share God's love. As you post, affirm, "I share this post with great love for all who notice it."

Social Media Affirmations

In the spirit of Therese of Lisieux, let I Thessalonians 5:16–18 guide your Internet and social media involvements:

Rejoice always, pray without ceasing, give thanks in

all circumstances; for this is the will of God in Christ Jesus for you.

You may want to write this passage on a note card to read throughout the day, especially in your social media activities. You may also create Internet affirmations based on I Thessalonians 5:16–18, such as:

I rejoice in all circumstances.

I give thanks throughout the day for the opportunity to share my thoughts on social media.

I pray every moment of the day and surround my social media communication with prayer.

I am aligned with God's will and follow God's guidance in all my social media communications.

Embody these affirmations by pausing to pray for Divine guidance, wisdom, and compassion as you begin each task throughout the day, as well as when you write an e-mail or post on social media. Soon a prayerful attitude will become your normal response to life's ups and downs. Interruptions will call you to prayer and invite you to serve in the spirit of Jesus. Without thinking, you will spread little flowers of love throughout your relationships and social media communications.

Prayer of Awareness and Transformation

Holy God, let me whole life be a prayer. Let the ordinary become a window to Divinity. Let my words and meditations, my acts and responses, bring healing and wholeness to the world. In Christ's name. Amen.

Seven

SOMETHING BEAUTIFUL FOR GOD
Teresa of Calcutta

Truly I tell you, just as you did it to one of the least of these who are members of my family, you did it to me.

(Matthew 25:40)

Seeking the face of God in everything, everyone, and everywhere, all the time, and seeing his hand in every happening—that is contemplation in the heart of the world.[22]

Our calling is simply "to do something beautiful for God."[23]

(Mother Teresa)

*D*o something beautiful for God! According to philosopher Alfred North Whitehead, the aim of the universe is toward the production of beauty. God seeks truth, beauty, and goodness both in our moment-by-moment experiences and in the long-term moral arc of the universe.

> **Never worry about numbers. Help one person at a time and always start with the person nearest you.**[24]
>
> (Mother Teresa)

Beauty involves the right blend of order and novelty, tradition and innovation, unity and complexity, all of which combine to contain depth of experience in the present moment and for the personal and global future.

We can't always define beauty. But we know it when we experience it—in a piece of music, a sunset over the Rockies, sunrise on Cape Cod, a child's frolicking, a lover's touch, falling snow, and starry nights. Beauty surrounds us, enlivening and enlightening, opening doorways to Divinity at every turn.

One of the challenges of social media relationships today is to remember that our primary goal in communication is to add to the beauty and goodness of the world. Rumi is right to say: "Let the beauty we love be what we do. There are hundreds of ways to kneel and kiss the ground."[25] We can be God's companions in beauty-making in many ways, ranging from comforting to challenging, inspiring to investigating, and singing to supporting.

I seek to bring beauty and healing to every interaction, including my social media activities. I must confess that beauty-making requires a great deal of mindfulness and self-knowledge. I can easily get off track, forgetting my spiritual goals, if I am ensnared by a position different from my own or find myself outraged at blatant untruths. Although I cultivate equanimity in my relationships and work, I experience a sense of agitation at such perversions of truth. My understanding of reality is being threatened. Once again, I want to the set the perpetrator straight and challenge the individual to go from darkness to my light. But then I remember that my goal is to build bridges of communication and not walls of division. I am reminded that deep down, there is, as the Quakers say, "something of God" in everyone and that I have a vocation to midwife the Divinity of others in terms of their own spiritual DNA and not my understanding of their ideal personhood. I am also reminded that in this grand universe, there is more than one right answer to many questions and that it is best to frame differing viewpoints in terms of "contrast," an aesthetic term, than "opposition," a militaristic term. This, of course, doesn't mean that I accept

> **The best way to show my gratitude to God is to accept everything, even my problems, with joy.**
>
> *(Mother Teresa)*

untruth and leave falsehood unchallenged—but I pick the right times, what the Gospels call the "kairos" moments, to share my contrasting visions of truth and beauty.

In our time, Mother Teresa of Calcutta (1910–1997), canonized as Saint Teresa in 2016, embodies our ability to discover beauty in what others see as ugliness and deformity. In her late thirties, Mother Teresa received a "call within a call" to "come, be my light," working with the most destitute of Calcutta, the vulnerable, impoverished, and dying, discarded ones, alone on the streets. In her own words, "I felt that God wanted from me something more. He wanted me to be poor with the poor."[26] In the final hours of people's lives, Mother Teresa sought to bring something of beauty to their lives:

> We want them to feel that they are wanted. . . . We want them to know that there are people who really love them, who really want them, at least for the few hours they have to live, to know human and divine love.[27]

Despite her generosity of spirit, Mother Teresa was accused of proselytizing the dying, trying to convert them in their final hours to Roman Catholicism. Her response was that conversion is personal and God's work in accordance with each person's deep spiritual needs and not our preconceived notions of salvation.

> I do convert. . . . I do convert you to be a better Hindu, a better Catholic, a better Muslim, or Jain or Buddhist. I would like to help you to find God. When you find Him, it is up to you to do what you want with Him.[28]

In the final years of her life, Mother Teresa saw the face of God in persons dying of AIDS. Scorned by friends and family, judged as sinners by religious leaders and those who presumed themselves to be righteous, they were to Mother Teresa simply God's beloved children, revealing the face of God where others saw sinfulness. Perhaps, Mother Teresa, who experienced the dark night of Divine absence throughout her ministry, knew that God is often most present when we feel most bereft. She could identify with, and universalize, the words of the apostle Paul, who faced his own chronic thorn in the flesh, despite his mystical encounters with God:

> **For love to be real, it must cost, it must hurt, it must empty us of self.**
>
> *(Mother Teresa)*

> God said to me, "My grace is sufficient for you, for power is made perfect in weakness." So, I will boast all the more gladly of my weaknesses, so that the power of Christ may dwell in me. Therefore I am content with weaknesses, insults, hardships, persecutions, and calamities for the sake of Christ; for whenever I am weak, then I am strong. (2 Corinthians 12:9–10)

Mother Teresa's own spiritual struggles became doorways to Divinity. She did not perceive herself superior to those whom she served. She was one with them, training her eyes for Christ in Christ's distressing disguises and then bringing forth beauty one encounter at a time: "Seeking the face of God in everything, everyone, and everywhere, all the time, and seeing

> **Joy is a net of love by which we catch souls.**
>
> (Mother Teresa)

his hand in every happening—that is contemplation in the heart of the world."

Alignment with truth, beauty, and goodness is a matter of choice, not emotion. Regardless of how we feel, or what triggers our feelings of anger and distaste, we need to recall our ultimate goals in every encounter. Mother Teresa had to transcend her experiences of Divine absence, the dark night of the soul. I need to transcend my visceral judgment of conservative Christians aligning themselves with what I perceive to be "godless" governmental policies and leaders. As Mother Teresa notes: "Thank God, we don't serve God with our feelings. Otherwise I don't know where I would be."30 Internet spirituality is a matter of choice, not emotion.

We choose to be faithful to God in all our interactions, especially with those with whom we disagree. In my faithfulness, I may choose to share my truth, but not with a desire to convert others to my way of thinking. I need to present my truth as an option, one I believe in and that is, as far as I can tell, worthy, insightful, and fact based. But, like our prayers, the moment I send a note off or say a prayer, I must let go of the outcome. In seeking to do something beautiful for God, I must allow the recipients of my prayers and counsel to discern where God is currently leading them, knowing that the path ahead is always mysterious and full of surprises.

> **If you judge people you have no time to love them.**
>
> (Mother Teresa)

As I write these words, the United States is in the middle of a political upheaval. The presidency of Donald Trump has caused battle lines to be drawn, and on social media, the political temperature is rising. I am fortunate to have a handful of friends who support the presidency and policies of Donald Trump. Did I say "fortunate"? Yes. I vehemently disagree with their apparently uncritical support of someone unworthy of the office of president of the United States. I have difficulty seeing the holiness of Donald Trump and find his policies dangerous and diabolical. I find any support of Trump incomprehensible given his character and actions. And yet Mother Teresa reminds me to see Christ in Christ's distressing disguises everywhere, even in the White House. My sense of the holiness of my own Facebook friends, some of whom I have known for nearly fifty years, allows me to stay in conversation. To critique and challenge them, and hear their responses, without dismissing or judging them. To pray for Donald Trump without condoning his behavior or policies. My friends and I have a thread of common history and decency that allows us to see our contrasting positions while respecting one another and recognizing our common ground.

Before you speak, it is necessary for you to listen, for God speaks in the silence of the heart.

(Mother Teresa)

While it is unlikely that Mother Teresa regularly took to the Internet and social media, her spiritual guidance is clear. Look for Christ in every social media companion, most especially those you are tempted to disregard as inferior or other than yourself. Open your eyes to the Christ within you and the Christ-Spirit joining you and your social media companions.

FINDING GOD ON THE INTERNET
Something Beautiful for God

God is online with you. God seeks beauty of holiness and wholeness in our daily lives and social media communications. Mother Teresa reminds us to look beyond the often-appalling behaviors we observe in public life and on social media, not succumbing to vitriol or abandoning the truth that we can see Christ beneath the distressing behaviors of our social media companions.

Seeing Christ in Others

Mother Teresa believed that the Living Christ was present deep down in everyone, especially those who distress and offend us. These persons are our spiritual teachers challenging us to see the inner Divinity that is often unknown to them. Each of us is carrying burdens that can get in the way of our experiencing our identity as God's beloved children. Still, there is a Divine restlessness moving within our lives, calling us—if we listen—to abundant life and deeper community, and calling us in every communication, even difficult ones, to become agents of wholeness and beauty.

In seeing Christ in the unexpected other—the one who is most unlike us or pushes all our emotional buttons—we are liberated to become God's healers in the world. Our lives, then, become ways we bring beauty and healing to God's experience of the world. In responding to the difficult persons we encounter on social media, we discover the place where Christ invites us to open our eyes and see hidden holiness.

Let us seek to look behind the Divine disguises to see God's presence in the politician we love to hate, the obnoxious stranger on Facebook, and the challenging people in our lives. Ask God to give you vision and help you respond in a way that brings life, rather than death or alienation. Let us breathe deeply and visualize Christ speaking to us through them.

Doing Something Beautiful for God

Mother Teresa counsels us, "Let's do something beautiful for God." In the spirit of her role model Therese of Lisieux, she saw each moment as an opportunity to choose life by doing ordinary things in a loving manner. When we act with love, we bring beauty to the world, aligning ourselves with God's universal aim at beauty. God has given us the task of being Divine companions in creativity and beauty-making, doing what only we can do as God's messengers in our moment-by-moment encounters. In focusing on the hidden beauty of others, we may become catalysts for them to experience their own beauty and holiness on God's terms and not our own!

Wisdom and insight can emerge from Facebook memes. This morning I saw the following on my Facebook page—a quote from President Jimmy Carter, reminiscent of John Wesley, was attached to his photo:

> I have one life and one chance to make it count for something. . .
> My faith demands that I do whatever I can,
> Wherever I can,
> Whenever I can,
> For as long as I can, with whatever I have
> To try to make a difference.

This is wisdom that guides our spiritual journey, whether we are president of the United States, building a house with Habitat for Humanity, tutoring a child at a local elementary school, making sandwiches for persons experiencing homelessness, or posting on social media. Always do something beautiful for God wherever Providence places you.

In the spirit of Sufi spiritual guide Rumi, there are hundreds of ways to bring beauty to the world. In a time of cultural divisiveness, we can bring beauty to the world by greeting a Muslim family at a restaurant, standing beside a woman with a hijab at the gas station when a stranger makes an unkind remark, or welcoming a foreign-visa student working for the summer at a local restaurant or supermarket. We can say a kind word online, remembering someone's birthday, sharing a word of gratitude with a former professor or spiritual guide, affirming a child's achievement.

Beauty is all around us. But we need to open our senses to it. We need, in the spirit of the Navajo Blessing Way, to affirm "with beauty all around me, I walk." We need to pause, notice, and bring forth beauty in our midst.

Take time each day to ask God to open your senses to beauty all around you. Ask God to help you see beyond the lampshade to notice the inner light of others and beyond the belligerence to see the hidden beauty in those who push your buttons. You can go through the day repeating, "My goal is to do something beautiful for God wherever I am" and then add beauty through helpful and loving acts.

Prayer of Awareness and Transformation

Loving God, open my senses to the beauty around me. Help me to look beyond appearances to see the Inner Christ. Guide me to do something beautiful for you in every encounter throughout the day. Amen.

Eight

PAUSE, NOTICE, OPEN, AND RESPOND

Gerald May

"Be still, and know that I am God! I am exalted among the nations, I am exalted in the earth." The Lord of hosts is with us; the God of Jacob is our refuge.

(Psalm 46:10–11)

He said, "Go out and stand on the mountain before the Lord, for the Lord is about to pass by." Now there was a great wind, so strong that it was splitting mountains and breaking rocks in pieces before the Lord, but the Lord was not in the wind; and after the wind an earthquake, but the Lord was not in the earthquake; and after the earthquake a fire, but the Lord was not in the fire; and after the fire a sound of sheer silence. When Elijah heard it, he wrapped his face in his mantle and went out and stood at the entrance of the cave. Then there came a voice to him that said, "What are you doing here, Elijah?"

(1 Kings 19:11–13)

In opening to the contemplative presence, we must finally come to clarity about the natural, graced balance and rhythm of stretching and yielding. One might say that contemplative prayer is nothing other than consecrated openness of stretching and yielding . . . think of stretching as reaching and opening, and yielding as acceptance and letting-be. Stretching is the self-claiming dimension; yielding is the welcoming dimension. Stretching is hopeful aspiration; in it the power of our selfhood is expressed. Yielding is like helpful hospitality; in it the dignity of our selfhood is expressed.[31]

(Gerald May)

Discovering God online involves listening to your life and letting your life speak, as Frederick Buechner and Parker Palmer counsel in their books. We need to stop long enough to still the constantly moving monkey mind and the knee-jerk "gotcha" response to claim our freedom to respond from a place of peace, reconciliation, and healing. Like Elijah, we need to pause long enough to transcend the maelstrom of diverse and divisive voices to listen for God's voice in "sheer silence." In the spirit of Psalm 46, we need to "be still," making room for the God who provided in the past to continue to provide for our deepest needs. I am constantly reminded to follow the wisdom of God, seeking to find the truth beneath my self-interest, anxiety, and combativeness:

> Likewise the Spirit helps us in our weakness; for we do not know how to pray as we ought, but that very Spirit intercedes with sighs too deep for words. And God, who searches the heart, knows what is the mind of the Spirit,

because the Spirit intercedes for the saints according to the will of God. (Romans 8:26–27)

God is constantly moving in our lives, deep within the unconscious as well as in the consciously apprehended events of our lives, guiding us toward wholeness and reconciliation. God's voice comes within the multitude of inner and outer voices that constantly influence us. God is here, but we need to declutter our spirits to receive God's graceful guidance.

Gerald May (1940–2005), psychiatrist and spiritual guide, shares a pattern of prayer that joins the inner and outer journeys. Put simply, May invites us to "pause, notice, open, yield, and stretch" to discern God's vision for our lives.[33] I have added "respond" to highlight more explicitly the importance of spiritual activism.

> **Many of the old understandings to which I had been addicted were stripped away, leaving a desertlike spaciousness where my customary props and securities no longer existed. Grace was able to flow into this emptiness, and something new was able to grow.**[32]
>
> *(Gerald May)*

The first step is *pausing*, standing quietly on the mountain top as God passes by. We can experience a grace note in our lives through gentle breathing.

In the second step, *noticing* our environment, the sounds, sights, and smells, and then going deeper to observe your body, emotional life, inner dialogue, and state of mind, until you discover your deepest desire of the moment.

Third, *opening* to the fullness of your experience, consecrating it and offering it to God in the words of a hymn I learned at childhood revival meetings, "Just as I am without one plea."

Fourth, *yielding* to the moment in its fullness and God's movements in your life, setting aside your ego to listen to the fullness of Divinity in your finite experience. Yielding is the acceptance of what *is* in this holy moment.

The facts of grace are simple: grace always exists, it is always available, it is always good, and it is always victorious.[34]

(Gerald May)

Fifth, *stretching* toward God with all of your agency, seeking to align your will with God's will, acting alongside God, accepting Divine guidance and inspiration.

Finally, *responding* to your experience with as much stature and inclusiveness as possible, letting your life speak to transform the world "on earth as it is in heaven."

In this process, inner and outer meet, and our actions find their grounding in Divine creativity and wisdom. We recognize our weakness and finitude. We also experience our deepest reality as being a little lower than the angels (Psalm 8). I believe that God addresses

Mysterious as it may be, there is something wonderful at the heart of our existence, and it is about nothing other than love; love for God, love for one another, love for creation, love for life itself.[35]

(Gerald May)

us in every encounter—and that when we let go of our ego, our need to be right, we can become God's companions in healing and wholeness. Each moment comes with a message, and when we pause, notice, open, yield, and stretch, God works with us to respond in ways that bring wholeness and comfort and joy. Attentive to God's deeper wisdom, we can discover ourselves on holy ground, even as we post, tweet, or respond to posts.

FINDING GOD ON THE INTERNET
Pause, Notice, Open, and Respond

Civility in everyday life and social media is grounded in self-awareness and self-control, knowing who you are, your temptations and talents, and the importance of graceful restraint. I find wisdom in a song written by Dan Schlitz and popularized by Kenny Rogers: "You've got to know when to hold 'em and know when to fold 'em"—and when to simply walk away from the table and refuse to play the game any longer. Relational grace is grounded in our awareness of our fallibility and limitations, as well as the holiness of those with whom we interact.

Living with the Jesus Prayer

In one of his books, Gerald May cites the fourth-century Jesus Prayer as a constant companion in our spiritual journey: *Jesus, Son of the Living God, have mercy on me a sinner.* The origins of this "prayer of the heart" are to be found in scripture—sight-impaired Bartimaeus's cry for healing: "Jesus, Son of David, have mercy on me!" (Mark 10:46–52), and the tax collector's prayer: "God be merciful to me, a sinner!" (Luke 18:9–14).

Gracefulness inspires humility, our sense of dependence on a Holy Wisdom and Power, a Love, greater than ourselves, and our constant need for Divine guidance and support. Or, in the spirit of another hymn I learned in childhood: "It's me, it's me, it's me, O Lord, standin' in the need of prayer." The Jesus Prayer reminds us of our finitude and fallibility, as well as the grandeur of our heartfelt prayer.

As I am aware of the graceful and universal interdependence that connects our world, I am better able to recognize the wisdom counseled by theologian Reinhold Niebuhr: to recognize the truth in my neighbor's falsehood and the falsehood in my own truth. I carry this advice with me whenever I am tempted to use my intellectual or spiritual "superiority" to challenge another's belief. The distance between saint and sinner and wise and foolish is much less than we think. Prophetic challenge reconciles only when it comes from a place of humility and confession.

In this exercise, throughout the day, make the Jesus prayer your companion, whether in a simple form such as "God have mercy on me" or an extended form, "Lord Jesus, Son of the Living God, have mercy on me a sinner." Recite this prayer as you log on and whenever you are tempted to enter the fray on social media.

Consecrating the Moment

Throughout the day and as you sign on to the Internet or your social media account, take a few moments for the spiritual practice highlighted in this chapter:

- *Pause:* Take a few deep breaths, visualizing yourself inhaling God's Spirit and exhaling any stress or anxiety you may be experiencing.
- *Notice:* What do you see online? What is its impact on you emotionally? What responses is it evoking?
- *Open:* Embrace the fullness of your experience, including God's presence in your life.
- *Stretch:* Reach out toward God's guidance and wisdom.
- *Yield:* Listen and accept God's wisdom in this moment.
- *Respond:* Your response may be the Jesus Prayer, a spiritual affirmation, some deep centering breaths, or a prayer for someone you encounter online. It may simply to be still rather than comment, recognizing that you and your respondent are both in God's care.

Heavy on my heart as I wrote today was a Facebook post from the daughter of a schoolmate from the class of 1970, who is returning to the hospital for treatment for a recurrence of leukemia. I didn't know her mother well in high school, but her post called me to respond. I felt guided to share my faith and offer my prayers and a form of energy healing—Reiki healing touch, prayer with your hands, from a distance. I want to be an instrument of peace wherever I find myself, and today God was present online calling me to be "on the side of the angels," to share the energy of love to a companion in need. For those with eyes to see and ears to hear—and senses to intuit—the posts we read can be calls to healing conversations and prayerful posts. We can, in the spirit of Mary Oliver, pay attention, be astonished, and speak out about our experience.[36]

Prayer of Awareness and Transformation

Loving God, let me remember both my grandeur and sin, my gifts and my limitations, that I might respond toward others with grace and humility. Amen.

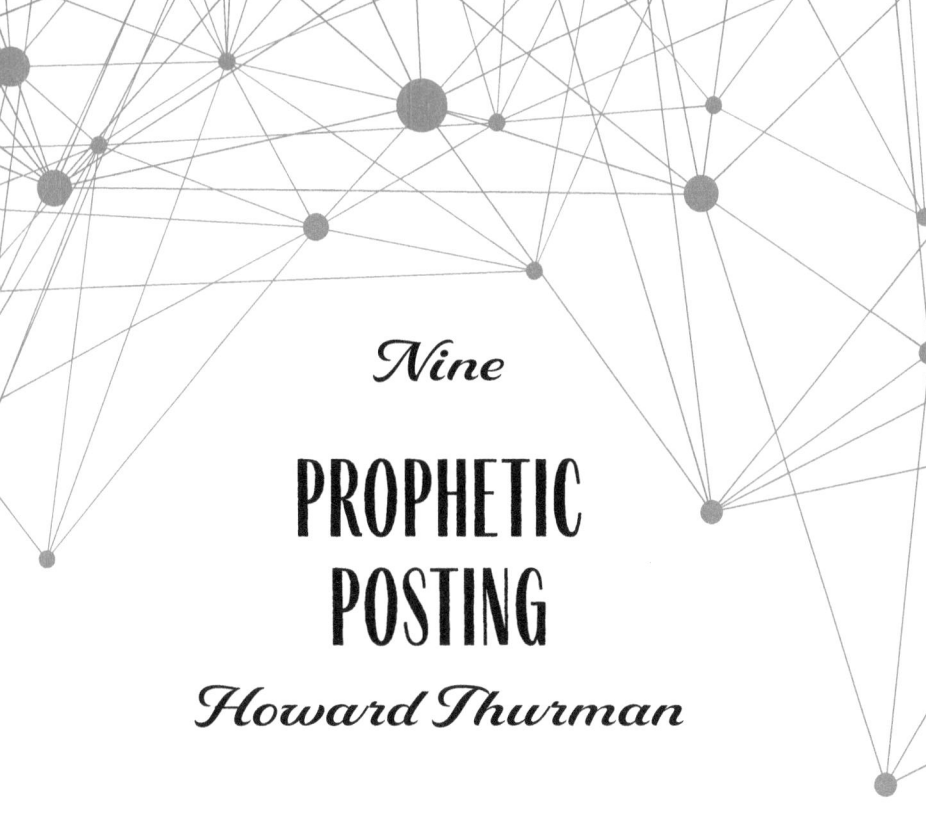

Nine

PROPHETIC POSTING

Howard Thurman

In the year that King Uzziah died, I saw the Lord sitting on a throne, high and lofty; and the hem of his robe filled the temple. Seraphs were in attendance above him; each had six wings: with two they covered their faces, and with two they covered their feet, and with two they flew. And one called to another and said: "Holy, holy, holy is the Lord of hosts; the whole earth is full of his glory."

The pivots on the thresholds shook at the voices of those who called, and the house filled with smoke. And I said: "Woe is me! I am lost, for I am a man of unclean lips, and I live among a people of unclean lips; yet my eyes have seen the King, the Lord of hosts!"

Then one of the seraphs flew to me, holding a live coal that had been taken from the altar with a pair of tongs. The seraph touched my mouth with it and said: "Now that this has touched your lips, your guilt has departed and your sin is blotted out." Then I heard the voice of the Lord saying, "Whom shall I send, and who will go for us?" And I said, "Here am I; send me!"

(Isaiah 6:1-8)

The place where imagination shows its greatest power as the agent of God is in the miracle which it creates, when one [person] . . . is able, while remaining there, to put [awareness] in another's place.... All [people] belong to each other, and [those] who shut [themselves] away diminish [themselves], and [those] who shut another away from them destroy [themselves].[37]

(Howard Thurman)

When I was growing up, religion and politics were off limits for polite conversation. They were reserved for church and political meetings. People seldom spoke about mystical and paranormal experiences or their spiritual commitments, except in theosophical and holy-roller circles. Today, religion and politics are out in the open, especially on social media. People argue and denounce each other over issues such as who is a true progressive or the heartlessness of the U.S. immigration policy. Critiques of the hypocrisy of evangelicals supporting Donald Trump and the heretical tendencies of progressive Christians abound. Even Buddhists, Hindus, and Muslims snipe at each other about rituals, ethics, and the nature of salvation. On occasion, someone shows up on my thread, denouncing my audacity to take matters of faith seriously. Humans are profoundly social animals, and our community orientation manifests in sharing our political and religious commitments. Even when we denounce another, we are expressing our connectedness, albeit in an unhealthy way.

Even mystics can't avoid facing the challenges of religion and politics; although they relied on private moments of contemplation, they did not remove themselves totally from the world. Tradition has it, for example, that the anchorite cell of Julian of Norwich (1342–1416) had two windows: one faced the Norwich Cathedral's sanctuary and the sacraments, the other faced the street, allowing her to glean news from the wider world and provide spiritual counsel to passersby. Even Thomas Merton, who spent much of his life isolated in the Trappist monastery at Gethsemane, Kentucky, spoke of the "conjectures of a guilty bystander," referring to his thoughts on the political and social arena of his day.

Our own experience is similar. The dynamic, interdependent, and noospheric nature of life, enhanced by the immediacy of the Internet, social media, and the 24/7 news cycle, joins us as one planetary community, despite the individualistic and nation-first philosophies of some of us. There is truly nowhere to run and nowhere to hide, even when we attempt to go off the grid.

> **There is something in every one of you that waits and listens for the sound of the genuine in yourself. It is the only true guide you will ever have. And if you cannot hear it, you will all of your life spend your days on the ends of strings that somebody else pulls.**[38]
>
> *(Howard Thurman)*

The planetary noosphere challenges us to move from ignorance and apathy to awareness and empathy, in which we persons of faith are challenged to hear the groans of creation and the cries of the poor. The spiritual noosphere invites us to embrace diverse forms of prophetic spirituality and explore alternatives to isolating individualism, consumerism, injustice, and planetary destruction. The heat that often eclipses the light in social media conversations invites us to explore a new spiritual vocation, that of prophetic healing, a place where honesty, challenge, and peace embrace one another.

One of my spiritual mentors Howard Thurman (1899–1981) points us toward the pathway of prophetic healing in our time, protests grounded in prayer and challenges leading to community.[40] Howard Thurman grew up in the Jim Crow era, in which "separate but equal" meant inequality for African Americans, and danger lurked whenever a person of color crossed the lines determined by the sensibilities of the white community. In Florida, where Thurman grew up, persons of color had few educational opportunities—but through grace, grit, and the force of will of his mother and grandmother, Thurman attended the finest schools in the United States, and grew into a renowned writer, education, pastor, and university spiritual leader. Still, he always knew that he was African American in the United States of

> The movement of the Spirit of God in the hearts of men and women often calls them to act against the spirit of their times or causes them to anticipate a spirit which is yet in the making. In a moment of dedication they are given wisdom and courage to dare a deed that challenges and to kindle a hope that inspires.[39]
>
> *(Howard Thurman)*

America, subject to abuse, discrimination, and hate, despite his professional achievements. He wisely noted in his *Jesus and the Disinherited*, perhaps the first book published in black liberation theology, that as the citizen of an occupied land, Jesus never had a moment of freedom. Like others who have their backs against the wall, Jesus had to discover a pathway of transcendence that enabled him to challenge authority while recognizing that the oppressor is also a child of God.

An incident from Thurman's childhood reveals the psychological and spiritual roots of incivility, objectification, and diminishment. One autumn, young Howard worked a for a white store owner, raking leaves. After he raked them in a pile, the store owner's four-year-old daughter decided to play a game. Whenever she saw a brightly colored leaf, she scattered the whole pile to show it to Howard. She did this several times until Howard lost his patience and told her to stop. When she continued, he threatened to tell her father about her mischief-making. Angry at his reprimand, the young girl jabbed him with a straight pen. When he cried out, the girl responded, "O Howard, that didn't hurt you. You can't feel."[42]

You can't feel! Lack of empathy is at the heart of incivility. From this perspective, the other, the one who differs from me,

> **Jesus rejected hatred because he saw that hatred meant death to the mind, death to the spirit, and death to communion with his Father. He affirmed life; and hatred was the great denial.**[41]
>
> *(Howard Thurman)*

is truly "other," unable to feel the things that I feel. We have nothing in common, including our humanity. Experiences such as this one, often the result of thoughtlessness and social influence, shaped Thurman's vision of reality and his quest to liberate his people and all people. Thurman recognized that he, along with all persons of color in a racist society, would always be "an outsider in the community of power, where most of the life and death decisions are made which control the common life."[43] He knew he must always struggle to affirm his value as a child of God

> To love is to make of one's heart a swinging door.[45]
>
> (Howard Thurman)

as the foundation of challenging the injustices of his nation. Thurman realized that his spiritual liberation depended on finding "within myself the door that no man could shut, to locate resources that are uniquely mine, to which I must be true if the personal enterprise of my life is to be sustained despite the ravages inflicted upon it by society."[44]

With the Hebraic prophets, Thurman discovered that our encounter with God has social consequences. "Social action, therefore, is an expression of resistance against whatever tends to, or separates one, from the experience of God, who is the ground of [our] being."[46] Mysticism is not otherworldly but profoundly prophetic and political. "For the mystic, social action is sacramental, because it is not an end in itself. Always, it is the individual who must be addressed, located and released, underneath . . . misery and . . . hunger and . . . destitution. That whatever may be blocking [the] way to [the person's] own center where [the individual's] altar may be found, this

> There is a quiet courage that comes from an inward spring of confidence in the meaning and significance of life. Such courage is an underground river, flowing far beneath the shifting events of one's experience, keeping alive a thousand little springs of action.[48]
>
> (Howard Thurman)

must be removed."[47] Yet, although prophetic mysticism challenges the powerful, its intent is to liberate oppressor and oppressed to their common identity as God's beloved children, in a world in which all people deserve justice and abundant life.

The prophet Amos recognized that injustice harms the oppressor as well as the oppressed. Inability to hear the cries of the poor leads to spiritual malnourishment.

> Hear this, you that trample on the needy, and bring to ruin the poor of the land.... The time is surely coming, says the Lord God, when I will send a famine on the land; not a famine of bread, or a thirst for water, but of hearing the words of the Lord. They shall wander from sea to sea, and from north to east; they shall run to and fro, seeking the word of the Lord, but they shall not find it. (Amos 8:4, 11–12)

Speaking the truth with love, recognizing "something of God" in our Facebook and Twitter companions and political leaders with whom we disagree—these attitudes aim at wholeness and creative transformation, not destruction and diminishment. Protest is grounded in prayer and recognition that the oppressor, like us, can feel. Perhaps those whom we challenge will initially recognize that persons of goodwill see the world differently than they do. They may recognize in your irenic posts—the fact that you express your viewpoint without name-calling—a larger perspective and explore alternative understandings of political, ethical, and spiritual issues. They may discover that others truly feel pain, some of which may be the result of positions and politicians they support.

> What is important for the mystic is that the purpose of the shock treatment is to hold before the offender a mirror that registers an image of himself, that reflects the image of those who suffer at his hands. The total function of such action is to tear [people] from any alignments that prevent them from putting themselves in the other person's place, but it must never be forgotten that the central concern of the mystic is to seek to remove anything that prevents the individual from free and easy access to [the] own altarstair that is in [the person's] own heart.[49]

In developing his own inner life, through contemplation, prayer, and study, Thurman found the resources to transcend the injustices he and other African Americans daily experience, discover his own identity as God's beloved, and see that common holiness in oppressor and oppressed alike.

Vision is everything, whether on Facebook, Twitter, or any other social media app. Looking deeply, we discover our own hidden holiness and the hidden wholeness of others. My own quest to see the holiness of all people has led me to treat with respect those with whom I disagree, to learn about their personal projects and values, and discover what is important to them. Although I continue to object to their political and ethical viewpoints, I now see them from a larger, more compassionate perspective, which shapes my responses and often leads me to keep my thoughts to myself rather than needlessly attacking their position. I recognize the defensiveness and anxiety hidden behind their vitriol—and I know that only through relationship can we find a common ground for healthy conversation.

> **Whatever may be the tensions and the stresses of a particular day, there is always lurking close at hand the trailing beauty of forgotten joy or unremembered peace.**[50]
>
> *(Howard Thurman)*

FINDING GOD ON THE INTERNET
Prophetic Postings

Prophetic spirituality is grounded in empathy, going beyond objectification to experiencing the holiness of others in all their tragic beauty. Abraham Joshua Heschel describes God's relationship to humanity in terms of the Divine pathos—God's identification with human suffering and joy. Prophets experience the world through the lenses of Divine empathy, presenting an alternative reality to institutional, economic, and governmental injustice. In the biblical tradition, prophets have the audacity to speak for God, but their boldness is grounded in humility, the recognition of their imperfections and limitations countered by the confidence they gain in their encounters with the Holy One. Their recognition of their personal fallibility drives them to trust God and to transcend self-interest to focus on world loyalty and planetary healing. They recognize the whole Earth is full of God's glory, and the holiness of God's world includes those whom they challenge and critique. Prophets' messages, though sometimes painful, are a type of spiritual surgery intended to bring healing to the oppressor as well as the oppressed.

While we may not claim the vocation of social media prophets, our calling is to go beyond our egos to promote the well-being of all with whom we communicate and the world around us. We can share our truth, our own message of "thus saith the Lord," without demonizing those with whom we contend.

Seeing the Hidden Holiness

The integration of justice with compassion is grounded in our ability to see the hidden holiness of all people. As one of my colleagues counsels, we need to see the world with our "Jesus glasses" to experience the pain of the poor and the yearnings of the wealthy.

Look beyond appearances to see the Divinity of each person. Let your social media encounters be a laboratory for compassion, embracing, as the Buddhist sages say, all sentient beings, knowing that often belligerence and bloviation hide woundedness and fear. When you witness on social media a hateful or dishonest comment or meme, or a justification for injustice, let your compassionate perspective invite you to a few moments of spiritual archeology. Look at that person's page, peer at their photographs, and try to experience their life beyond their social media comments. They too may feel fear and pain!

Prayerfully seek to discern something of God within them, some glimmer of goodness and human-heartedness, as a reminder that you are encountering flesh-and-blood mortals—finite, fallible, possibly traumatized and fearful. Their values may differ from your own, but they too experience joy and pain, love and loneliness. You may still feel inspired to call them out for an untruth or challenge their perceptions of reality, but now your responses will come from the recognition of a common humanity.

In getting to know another online, you avoid polarization and objectification. You discover, in the experience of Howard Thurman, that they are real persons who can feel too, and that you can appeal to their higher self, whether you simply pray for God's presence in their lives or protest their value system.

Prophetic Prayerful Posting

Words matter. What we say and how we say it can bring healing light and promote common ground or widen the gulf between us? One of my personal affirmations is

"Let my words be truthful, loving, and healing," based on the psalmist's affirmation:

> May the words of my mouth and the meditation of my heart be acceptable to You, Lord, my rock and my Redeemer. (Psalm 19:14 HCSB)

Over the past few years, we have witnessed the consequences of verbal incivility in political debates and from the highest office of the United States of America. We have seen the power of words, even if not directly intended, to incite violence and hatred, at home and abroad.

Words can create or kill, heal or harm. As an African American growing up in the Jim Crow era and throughout his life, Howard Thurman knew the power of words. He knew that words are intended to be creative, but they can equally be demeaning, devasting, and destructive. I suspect Thurman sought to speak and write in accordance with the observations of the Epistle of James:

> Not many of you should become teachers, my brothers and sisters, for you know that we who teach will be judged with greater strictness. For all of us make many mistakes. Anyone who makes no mistakes in speaking is perfect, able to keep the whole body in check with a bridle. If we put bits into the mouths of horses to make them obey us, we guide their whole bodies. Or look at ships: though they are so large that it takes strong winds to drive them, yet they

are guided by a very small rudder wherever the will of the pilot directs. So also the tongue is a small member, yet it boasts of great exploits.

How great a forest is set ablaze by a small fire! And the tongue is a fire. The tongue is placed among our members as a world of iniquity; it stains the whole body, sets on fire the cycle of nature, and is itself set on fire by hell. For every species of beast and bird, of reptile and sea creature, can be tamed and has been tamed by the human species, but no one can tame the tongue—a restless evil, full of deadly poison. With it we bless the Lord and Father, and with it we curse those who are made in the likeness of God. From the same mouth come blessing and cursing. My brothers and sisters, this ought not to be so. Does a spring pour forth from the same opening both fresh and brackish water? Can a fig tree, my brothers and sisters, yield olives, or a grapevine figs? No more can salt water yield fresh. (3:1–12)

Let our prophetic posts be prayerful. Let us challenge injustice with truth, reason, and compassion. Before you post remember the words of the psalmist and the Epistle of James. Breathe deeply of Divine wisdom as you ask yourself: *Will these words inflame or heal? Will they promote creative conversation or destructive denunciation? Do I see the deeper spirit of the person I am challenging? Or are they merely an object to be attacked?* Prayerfully ask God to give you the wisdom to speak the truth with love.

Prayer of Awareness and Transformation

Loving God, you are the air we breathe, the ground upon which we walk, and the persons we meet today. Help us to see you in your most challenging disguises and call forth our compassion and advocacy for the poor, powerless, and disenfranchised. Amen.

Ten

WHAT IS YOUR VISION FOR YOUR UNIQUE AND UNREPEATABLE LIFE?

Mary Oliver

And on the seventh day God finished the work that God had done, and God rested on the seventh day from all the work that God had done. So God blessed the seventh day and hallowed it, because on it God rested from all the work that God had done in creation.

(Genesis 2:2–3)

You must not, ever, give anyone the responsibility for your life.[51]
(Mary Oliver)

Earlier in this book, I invoked the spiritual wisdom of Mary Oliver's question regarding our one wild and precious life. Theologian Paul Tillich might phrase Oliver's query in terms of "What is your ultimate concern?" Jesus might query, "Where is your treasure?" How we spend the time of our lives reveals what is truly important to us. Our values are reflected not only in our use of our talents and treasures but in how we use time. What will we do with the time of our life, moment by moment, hour by hour, and day by day? Will we fill our time with meaningless activities that deaden the spirit—or enterprises that add energy and zest to our lives?

According to the Celtic tradition, "thin places" are the intersection of God and the world in which earthly sites become transparent to Divinity. All space is holy and yet certain spaces reveal God's presence in unique and transformative ways. Jacob rests his head on a rock, dreams of a ladder of angels, and awakens, stammering in awe, "Surely the Lord is in this place, and I was not aware of it. . . . How awesome is this place! This is none other than the house of God; this is the gate of heaven" (Genesis 28:16–17 NIV). Some places stand out in revealing the Holy, and perhaps God chooses to be more present in some places than others. Still, if we affirm "God in all things and all things in God," then every place is a thin place for those who have their senses trained for Divinity.

In a similar fashion, the New Testament contrasts chronos and kairos time. Chronos time is the evenly moving tick-tock of everyday life and clock time. Kairos time points to the unique moments when God reveals Godself in saving ways. A God committed to this world's well-being is present in every moment, and yet ordinary moments can be windows into Divinity. Jesus is born in a manger, unnoticed by passersby. Only those who were touched by God saw Divinity in a humble stable. Discerning the intersection of "ordinary" chronos and kairos time, the right time for healing and transformation, is a matter of perception as well as Presence.

> **Do you think there is anything not attached by its unbreakable cord to everything else?**[52]
>
> *(Mary Oliver)*

In the Bible, when the faithful and unfaithful ask, "When did we see you?" it is evident that both are able to experience the same reality: God's presence in the hungry, thirsty, and naked. In the words of Elizabeth Barrett Browning, every time-place is God-filled for those whose senses are opened:

> Earth's crammed with heaven,
> And every common bush afire with God,
> But only he who sees takes off his shoes;
> The rest sit round and pluck blackberries.

Burning bushes and incarnations are everywhere, but we need to pause long enough to notice Divine revelations on the way to work or when we log onto the Internet.

Studies suggest that the average Internet user spends two hours each day on some form of social media or Internet activity. Many of us pass a coast-to-coast plane trip on Candy Crush, Fortnite Battle Royale, Mindcraft, or Madden Football, or we play a word game, such as Word Scape, prior to retiring at night. At any given time, over five million people are playing Fortnite Battle Royale. Can you imagine it—spending the equivalent of thirty days online each year or seven or eight years over a lifetime? Our attachment to online entertainment has led comedian-commentator Bill Maher to quip: "Philip Morris just wanted your lungs. The App Store wants your soul."[54]

Attention is the beginning of devotion.[53]

(Mary Oliver)

The ubiquitous 24/7 presence of social media has led computer scientist Cal Newport to become an advocate for "digital minimalism" described as:

> A philosophy of technology use in which you focus your online time on a small number of carefully selected and optimized activities that strongly support things you value, and then happily miss out on everything else.[55]

In the spirit of Mary Oliver's caution that we not "give away" our responsibility for our own lives, Newport advises us to focus on our deepest values and align our social media activities accordingly. With the temporal spaciousness created by reducing our connections to social media and Internet gaming, we have more time for walking, reading, life entertainment, relationships, prayer, and contemplation.

Newport rightly notes the addictive lure of social media. This is true for computer video games as well as constant scrolling of Facebook posts, not to mention posting. What begins as a pastime can take up your whole daytime and get in the way of creativity and personal growth. On a lighter note, in describing our contemporary attachments to our cell phones, a friend recently told me about a comic strip that pictured Saint Peter's observing a group of newcomers to heaven. The saint was perplexed when after welcoming recent arrivals at the pearly gates, they began staring at their empty hands. "What are they doing?" Saint Peter asked his angelic assistant, who responded, "They think they're looking at their cell phones!"

> So quickly, without a moment's warning, does the miraculous swerve and point to us, demanding that we be its willing servant.[56]
>
> (Mary Oliver)

How will you spend your one amazing and radiant life? Will you just visit the world, never connecting with the depths of reality and God's revelation in everyday relationships? Will your life be defined in terms of virtual reality—or will you discover that each morning and every encounter, including every post, is Beth-El, the pathway to heaven on earth?

The biblical notion of Sabbath presents an alternative approach to life. Time-space is the sanctuary of life, the temple of the Holy Spirit, and the crucible of Divine activity. God is constantly creating, and God's mercies are new every morning. Behold, each moment brings something new in God's quest for beauty, justice, and community. Each moment is filled with possibilities, but as Ecclesiastes avers, there is a time for every season under heaven. There is time for activity and time for rest. Time for protest and time for prayer. Time for social media and time for face-to-face conversation. Time for video games and time for physical activity. A time for the Internet and a time for Nature. Time for high tech and time for high touch. As Jesus' ministry reveals, Sabbath time is open-spirited, guided by the Spirit who goes where she wills, not bound by legalism. Still, rhythm is essential to our spiritual growth. We need a variety of Sabbaths to define and transform our days, weeks, months, and years.

> **We are built of light, and God is within us.**[57]
>
> *(Mary Oliver)*

In my own life, I follow what I call a crop-rotation approach to work and play. I seldom do any activity—whether writing a book, lecture, or sermon; making pastoral phone calls or visits; or connecting with the Internet—for more than forty-five minutes at a time. When I go from one activity to the next, I pause and take a few breaths, invoking God's presence when I inhale and letting go of stress or my previous focus as I exhale. I have found that this crop-rotation approach keeps me fresh throughout the day and connects a variety of disparate activities with my ultimate life goal to experience God's presence and bless others.

Of course, there are times when I must hunker down on a project for several hours or get caught up in social media posts or blogging. Even in these activities, however, I pause long enough to breathe deeply, rise from my Arts-and-Crafts recliner chair, set aside my computer, and spend a few minutes interacting with my wife or going out into the garden to embrace the beauty of our home. I am fortunate that I have freedom to choose much of my schedule. This enables me to set aside social media, writing, and work activities when my grandchildren are with me at home or on a neighborhood adventure, or when I walk the beach with my wife Kate and our golden doodle Tucker.

Presence is at the heart of spirituality, and our children and grandchildren remind us graphically of the fleeting nature of life. Turn around, and an infant is a toddler; close your eyes, and they are in elementary school; daydream, and they are graduating from high school!

> **The universe is full of radiant suggestion.**[58]
>
> *(Mary Oliver)*

Many persons, including myself, take Internet and social-media Sabbaths or have learned to view Internet activity as a spiritual practice. I am currently trying to explore using the traditional practice of connecting my social media use with the traditional monastic practice of Praying the Hours. While I occasionally receive emergency messages to which I need to respond immediately, I have begun a practice of signing on to social media and the Internet after morning meditation (5:30 a.m.), midmorning (9:00 a.m.), prior to lunch (11:30 a.m.), midafternoon (2:00 p.m.), prior to dinner (5:30 p.m.), and early evening (7:30 p.m.). I connect these times with a moment of prayer, my own version of Praying the Hours, breathing deeply and opening to Divine wisdom or a more extended time of prayerful contemplation. I find this both concentrates and limits Internet use and makes my use of social media sacramental in spirit. It also reminds me that I don't need to be available 24/7; the world is ultimately in God's hands and not my own. If someone truly needs me, there is always my cell phone or a text message. Of course, I need to be judicious in responding to these as well. Every moment and ever encounter is holy—but not all encounters are urgent!

> **Wonderful things may happen if you break the ropes that are holding you.**[59]
>
> (Mary Oliver)

Internet and social-media Sabbaths are also essential to our personal well-being. While I am not legalistic about these weekly sabbaticals, I tend to log off on Saturdays before dinner and peek at my e-mail on Sunday mornings to be up on issue critical health issues among church members. I return to check my mail and scroll down my Facebook account briefly on Sunday afternoon. While I enjoy reading others' posts and like to share what's going in my own life, these hours of grace refresh my spirit and open my schedule for time with family and friends. Most days, the world can wait for my wisdom and insights!

The apostle Paul asserts that "all things are lawful, but not all things are beneficial. All things are lawful, but not all things build up" (1 Corinthians 10:23). That is the issue, isn't it? What behaviors deepen your relationship with God and others? What activities add beauty to the world, and promote well-being in the body politic? It has been said that at their deathbed, few people regret missing a meeting. Surely, the same is the case for the Internet and social media—when our days are numbered, few of us will lament missing an hour of Mindcraft or Candy Crush or failing to post on Facebook. Instead, we'll mourn missing our children's and grandchildren's childhood or intimate times with our loved ones. We may repent failing to seek justice, reaching out to the vulnerable, and caring for the planet.

In his counsel to the Corinth-ians, Paul advise that we live accor-ding to our deepest spiritual values and let our values guide how we use our time. Following our values will help us separate the wheat and the chaff, declutter our schedules, and enable us to do ordinary things, as Therese of Lisieux counsels, with great love. Our pace will be spacious and welcoming, not hurried and distracted. Our Internet and social media use, then, becomes a sanctuary of the spirit, a place for authentic relationship, sacred communication, and service to the world. Truly, we will experience God online!

> **We are each other's destiny.**[60]
>
> *(Mary Oliver)*

FINDING GOD ON THE INTERNET
Time for God

Our use of social media and time spent on the Internet reflects our values and priorities. Often these values are implicit and habitual, rather than intentional and healthy.

Without thinking, we sign in to Twitter, Facebook, or Instagram. While life can be spontaneous and playful, our play and novelty can reflect our deeper values and spiritual goals.

Time Examen

In this first exercise, set aside a period each evening or morning for a Time Examen. Over a week's period, reflect on how you spend your days—work, relaxation, reflection, study, exercise, and so forth. At the end of each day, find a quiet place for reflection, asking: *Was I living or visiting my life today? Did my use of time bring joy, beauty, meaning, or hope to myself and those around me? How much time did I spend on the Internet and social media? Was it satisfying? Did it add to the quality of my life? Am I happy and at peace with my daily activities? Did my daily routine bring me closer or further away from God's vision for my life?*

In response, take a few minutes to reflect on how you can live your life with greater intentionality and self-awareness. What first steps can you make to be more attentive to the Holy in the time of your life? What spiritual practices can awaken you to the spaciousness of God's presence in the world and your life?

Making Time Your Friend

Our use of the social media and the Internet reflects the totality of our lives. For many of us, time is scarce and flowing away from us. As the soap opera introduction notes, "Like sands in an hourglass, so go the days of our lives." Physician and spiritual guide Larry Dossey describes our modern attitude toward time as "hurry sickness." Like the White Rabbit in *Alice's Adventures in Wonderland*, we think of ourselves as "late, late, to a very important date," despite the fact that by day's end, we often look back and judge our hurry as misplaced and the event as trivial.

Promptness is a virtue. As a professional, I always intend to be early for every meeting. Still, I occasionally "stress out," when I thinking I'm running late, only to discover that I've arrived long before my companions.

Hurry is a state of mind, often caused by trying to do too many things in too little time or to many things at the same time—for example, I may find myself checking my voice mail, my e-mail, and responding to a text message. While many people boast of multitasking, studies suggest that persons who multitask are less efficient than those who focus on one thing at a time. "Deep work," as Cal Newport asserts, requires our full attention. As Ram Dass counseled, "Be here now" in this one amazing, unrepeatable God-filled moment.

Spiritual practices invite us to savor the moment and to be aware of the holiness of this present, fleeting, unrepeatable moment. Moving from hurried activity to calm activity is a matter of spiritual focus. In my own life, I regularly pause and assess my spiritual and emotional temperature, considering the following:

- Am I calm or anxious, interested or bored?
- Do I feel energized or weary?
- Do I perceive the people around me as companions on a journey or nuisances in the way?
- What is the quality of my interactions?
- Am I experiencing joy—or bliss, as Joseph Campbell writes—or unhappiness and depression?

You can do this time assessment in just a moment in the course of your day. It is more intuitive and experiential than analytic in nature. As a prelude to this exercise, take a moment to pause and breathe deeply as a centering practice. Visualize your inhaling in terms of the Spirit filling you with insight, energy, and inspiration. As you exhale, let go of any anxiety or sense of hurry, trusting the abundant Energy of Love undergirding all creation.

Internet and Social-Media Sabbath

At the heart of biblical spirituality is the interplay of rest and activity. For the Hebrews, the day began at sundown, at the end of the day when work was completed; rest, relaxation, and relationship were nocturnal priorities. In the Hebraic tradition, even God rests. God's sustaining of the universe is constant, and yet God creates a space for our creativity. God is not a micromanager or helicopter parent. God honors our freedom and artistry as Divine companions in healing the world.

Many families have found it helpful to reinstitute a version of Sabbath-keeping when it comes to social media and the Internet. My work as a pastor doesn't allow me to eliminate Internet and messaging entirely, even on weekends. In my vocation as a village pastor, I am on-call for deaths, accidents, and emergencies. However, from late afternoon on Saturday until Sunday after lunch, I create a Sabbath in which I do not initiate Internet conversations or scroll through my social media accounts. I focus on family life, especially time with our grandsons, who typically spend Saturday night at our home. I find this Sabbath a source of refreshment.

The Sabbath "sanctuary of time," as Abraham Joshua Heschel describes it, deepens our relationship to the Holy and makes all our days holy and spacious. Our commitment to Sabbath living is a sign that we trust God with the present and future and that our times are in God's hands. In seeing our Internet and social media as holy places and sanctuaries of time, we will truly experience God's presence. As Mary Oliver advised us, may we truly pay attention to every online encounter and post. In doing so, we may find ourselves astonished!

Prayer of Awareness and Transformation

God of all times and places, awaken me to Eternity in the midst of time. Bless my Internet interactions and social media posts. Help me to pay attention, and then let my words and meditations reflect your vision. Let them be sacramental in spirit, bringing holiness and connection to every encounter. Give me grace to let go and forgive; help me to choose the pathways of peace and healing when tempted to lash out in anger. May every moment be holy and loving, and every post reflect truth and compassion. May each moment be a holy adventure with you as my companion. Amen.

REFERENCE NOTES

1. Jean-Pierre de Caussade. *The Sacrament of the Present Moment* (New York: HarperSan Francisco, 1982). All quotations by de Caussade in this chapter are adapted from this book.
2. Brother Lawrence. *The Practice of the Presence of God* (New Kensington, PA: Whitaker House, 1982), 34.
3. Ibid., 23.
4. Unless otherwise indicated, all Brother Lawrence quotations are taken from *Brother Lawrence: A Christian Zen Master* (Vestal, NY: Anamchara Books, 2016).
5. Brother Lawrence. *The Practice of the Presence of God*, 93.
6. Frederick Buechner. *Secrets in the Dark: A Life in Sermons* (New York: HarperCollins, 2009), 20.
7. Frederick Buechner. *Now and Then* (San Francisco, CA: HarperOne, 1991).
8. Dale Brown. *The Book of Buechner: A Journey Through His Writings* (Louisville, KY: Westminster John Knox, 2007).
9. Mary Oliver. *Devotions: The Selected Poems of Mary Oliver* (New York, NY: Penguin, 2017), 316.
10. Ibid., 286.
11. This quote has been attributed to a number of thinkers, including Blaise Pascal, St. Bonaventure, Nicholas of Cusa, and Joseph Campbell. The earliest version of this quote apparently comes from Hermes Trismegistus, an ancient Greek philosopher.
12. Bernard Loomer. "S-I-Z-E Is the Measure," in Harry James Cargas and Bernard Lee, *Religious Experience and Process Theology* (Mahweh, NJ: Paulist Press, 1976), 70.
13. David J. Fleming, SJ. *The Spiritual Exercises of St. Ignatius: A Literal Translation and Contemporary Reading* (St. Louis, MO: The Institute of the Society of Jesus, 1980). All quotations from St. Ignatius's writings in this chapter are taken from this book.
14. Ibid., 62.

15. Thich Nhat Hanh. *Peace Is Every Step* (New York: Bantam Book, 1991). All quotations by Thich Nhat Hanh in this chapter are from this book, unless otherwise indicated.

16. As quoted in "Debasing Dissent" in the *New York Times* (16 November 1967), 46.

17. Sister Annabel Laity, editor. *Thich Nhat Hanh: Essential Writings* (Maryknoll, NY: Orbis, 2001), 58.

18. Joseph F. Schmidt. *Everything Is Grace: The Life and Way of Therese of Lisieux* (Frederick, MD: The Word Among Us Press, 2007), 198.

19. Ibid., 13.

20. Therese of Lisieux. *The Story of a Soul: The Autobiography of St. Therese of Lisieux* (Washington, DC: ICS Publications, 1996). All quotations by Therese in this chapter are from this book, unless otherwise indicated.

21. Schmidt, 20–21.

22. Kerry S. Walters. *St. Teresa of Calcutta: Missionary, Mother, Mystic* (Cincinnati, OH: Franciscan Media, 2016), 84.

23. Ibid., 89.

24. All quotations by Mother Teresa in this chapter, unless otherwise indicated, are from Crossroads, "Mother Teresa of Calcutta," https://www.crossroadsinitiative.com/saints/quotes-from-blessed-mother-teresa-of-calcutta/.

25. Coleman Barks. *The Essential Rumi* (San Francisco, CA: HarperSan Francisco, 1995), 36.

26. Walters, 27–29.

27. Ibid., 43.

28. Ibid., 43.

29. Ibid., 84.

30. Ibid., 255.

31. Gerald May. *The Awakened Heart: Opening Yourself to the Love You Need* (San Francisco, CA: HarperSan Francisco, 1991), 194.

32. Gerald May. *Addiction and Grace: Love and Spirituality in the Healing of Addictions* (New York: Harper Collins, 2009).

33. While May describes this process throughout *The Awakened Heart*, the best summary is found on pages 115–120.
34. May, *Addiction and Grace: Love and Spirituality in the Healing of Addictions*.
35. Gerald May. *The Dark Night of the Soul: A Psychiatrist Explores the Connection Between Darkness and Spiritual Growth* (Grand Rapids, MI: Zondervan, 2009), 6.
36. Mary Oliver. *Devotions: The Selected Poems of Mary Oliver* (New York: Penguin, 2017), 105.
37. Howard Thurman. *A Strange Freedom: The Best of Howard Thurman on Religion and the Public Life* (Boston, MA: Beacon Press, 1999), 248, 104.
38. Quoted in: Hazel Arnett Ervin and Lois Jamison Sheer, *A Community of Voices on Education and the African American Experience: A Record of Struggles and Triumphs* (Newcastle upon Tyne, UK: Cambridge Scholars Publishing, 2016), 326.
39. Howard Thurman. *Footprints of a Dream: The Story of the Church for the Fellowship of All Peoples* (New York: Harper, 1959), 7.
40. For more on my thoughts on Howard Thurman, see my book, *The Work of Christmas: The Twelve Days of Christmas with Howard Thurman* (Vestal, NY: Anamchara Books, 2017).
41. Howard Thurman. *Jesus and the Disinherited* (Boston, MA: Beacon Press, 2012), 88.
42. Howard Thurman. *With Heart and Mind* (New York: Harcourt Brace and Company, 1979), 12.
43. Howard Thurman. *Mysticism and Social Action: Lawrence Lectures and Discussions with Dr. Howard Thurman* (London: International Association for Religious Freedom, 2014), Kindle location 109.
44. Ibid., Kindle location 113–114.
45. Howard Thurman. *A Strange Freedom: The Best of Howard Thurman on Religious Experience and Public Life* (Boston, MA: Beacon Press, 2014), 184.
46. *Mysticism and Social Action*, Kindle location 235–236.

47. Ibid., Kindle location 249–251.

48. Howard Thurman. *Meditations of the Heart* (Boston, MA: Beacon Press, 2014), 52.

49. *Mysticism and Social Action*, Kindle location 270–274.

50. Howard Thurman. *Meditations of the Heart* (Boston, MA: Beacon Press, 2014), 211.

51. Mary Oliver. *Upstream* (New York: Penguin Press, 2016), 19.

52. Ibid., 5

53. Ibid., 8

54. Cal Newport. *Digital Minimalism: Choosing a Focused Life in a Noisy World* (New York: Penguin, 2019), 11.

55. Ibid., 28.

56. Upstream, 40.

57. Ibid., 108.

58. Ibid., 114.

59. Ibid.,145.

60. Ibid.,154

The 12 Days of Christmas with Bruce Epperly

Journey through the twelve days of Christmas with Bruce Epperly as your guide. Each of these books uses a different writer or way of thinking to form a structure that adds meaning and inspiration to the Season of Light.

Paperback Price: $10.99

Kindle Price: $5.99

Water from an Ancient Well
Celtic Spirituality for Modern Life

A Fresh Look at Celtic Spirituality

Using story, scripture, reflection, and prayer, this book offers readers a taste of the living water that refreshed the ancient Celts. The author invites readers to imitate the Celtic saints who were aware of God as a living presence in everybody and everything. This ancient perspective gives radical new alternatives to modern faith practices, ones that are both challenging and constructively positive. This is a Christianity big enough to embrace the entire world.

Paperback Price: $19.99

Kindle Price: $7.49

Become Fire!
Guideposts for Interspiritual Pilgrims

In the spirit of God's call to creative transformation, Bruce Epperly invites you to join him on a holy adventure in spiritual growth, inspired by the evolving wisdom of Christianity and the world's great spiritual traditions, innovative global spiritual practices, and emerging visions of reality. Epperly explores the many resources of Christian spirituality in dialogue with the spiritual practices of the world's great wisdom traditions, describing the gifts other spiritual paths contribute to the pathway of Jesus; at the same time, he uses the lens of the spiritual practices Jesus has inspired throughout Christian history to examine these spiritual paths. Epperly write as a Christian committed to Jesus, whose teachings and way of life he believes lead to pathways of healing and creative personal and planetary transformation. We need an illuminating and multifaceted spirituality, Epperly affirms, to shed light and provide guidance as we confront the unique crises of our time. By embracing the diverse insights of spiritual wisdom givers, physicists, cosmologists, healing practitioners, and Earth keepers, we can meet the Earth's current challenges with love, joy, and a united strength.

Paperback Price: $24.95

Kindle Price: $8.99

AnamcharaBooks.com